CLOUDS HILL

Charles Evered

BROADWAY PLAY PUBLISHING INC
56 E 81st St., NY NY 10028-0202
212 772-8334 fax: 212 772-8358
http://www.BroadwayPlayPubl.com

CLOUDS HILL
© Copyright 2004 by Charles Evered

First printing: December 2004
I S B N: 0-88145-257-2

Book design: Marie Donovan
Word processing: Microsoft Word
Typographic controls: Xerox Ventura Publisher 2.0 P E
Typeface: Palatino
Printed and bound in the U S A

ABOUT THE AUTHOR

Charles Evered is an author and journalist who has written; *The Size of the World and Other Plays*, (Billings/Morris, London, 1997), *The Shoreham and Other Plays*, (Whitman Press, 2002), ADOPT A SAILOR, (Emerson Review, 2003) and WILDERNESS OF MIRRORS, (Broadway Play Publishing Inc, 2004). Additional plays include; BOSTON, TED'S HEAD and LOOKING AGAIN.

CLOUDS HILL is the second play in his spy trilogy. The third play in the trilogy; CELADINE, premiered November of 2004 at The George Street Playhouse starring Amy Irving.

Mr Evered is a graduate of Rutgers, Yale University and The Naval Aviation Schools Command in Pensacola, Florida. He is a former officer in the United States Navy, (Res), having served with the Naval Office of Information during the onset of the War on Terror. Currently, he is an Assistant Professor at Emerson College in Boston. He is married to Wendy Rolfe Evered and the proud father of Margaret and John.

CLOUDS HILL was commissioned by The Manhattan
Theater Club in New York City with a grant from
the Alfred P Sloan Foundation. It was first presented
at M T C as a workshop on 1 August 2003 with the
following cast and creative contributor:

MICHAEL .... Rick Holmes
JANE .... Enid Graham
AHMAD .... Charles Daniel Sandoval

Director .... David Auburn

It was subsequently presented as a special presentation
at M T C on 1 December 2003 with the following cast
and creative contributor

MICHAEL .... David Harbour
JANE .... Mary Stuart Masterson
AHMAD .... Charles Daniel Sandoval

Director .... David Auburn

CLOUDS HILL was given its world premiere production at The City Lights Theater Company (Tom Gough, Artistic Director) in San Jose, California, opening September 18, 2004. The cast and creative contributors were:

MICHAEL .... Kit Wilder
JANE .... Lisa Mallette
AHMAD .... Kunal Prasad

Director .... Charles Evered
Assistant director .... Ana-Catrina Buchser
Scenic design .... Kit Wilder
Costume design .... Joanne Martin
Lighting .... Brendan Bartholomew
Stage manager .... Kevin Morgan Major

CHARACTERS & SETTING

MICHAEL, *late thirties/forties. A chemistry professor*
JANE, *a professor of political science. About the same age as*
  MICHAEL
AHMAD, *a student, early twenties*

The play takes place at Clouds Hill College, a small liberal arts college in the middle of the country.

The time is the present.

To Wendy Rolfe Evered;
Brilliant wife, brilliant mother, brilliant actress.
Thank you for walking up to me.

ACT ONE

(In the dark, we hear solo cello music and birds chirping. Lights bump up, revealing a woman sitting on a bench. A man stands behind her, saying nothing at first, then)

MICHAEL: I never talk to anyone I want to.

JANE: What?

MICHAEL: I walked across this entire green—thinking that up.

JANE: Did you? And what was it again?

MICHAEL: "I never talk to anyone I want to." I'm not saying it's "chisel worthy"....

JANE: You're the new chemistry guy.

MICHAEL: That's me.

JANE: Jane.

MICHAEL: Michael.

JANE: How do you like our little college so far? Is Clouds Hill everything you hoped it would be?

MICHAEL: What's not to like? Green grass, pastoral settings. And cookies. Cookies everywhere.

JANE: They're part of a plot.

MICHAEL: Really?

JANE: Yes, I have a theory about it. Would you like to hear it?

MICHAEL: I would—because I think I know where you're going.

JANE: I doubt it.

MICHAEL: You're right. That was presumptuous.

JANE: Here you are, after having negotiated—but only in a "representational" way, your salary. A salary that while you're not embarrassed of, still falls far short of both your expectations—but more importantly, your idea of "self."

MICHAEL: Nail on the head.

JANE: And now orientation week—they tell you where the gym is, they tell you how to take out a library book, they tell you "please—don't have sex with the students," and you're having buyer's remorse, aren't you? You're having second thoughts about having come here. You're having second thoughts about everything. About your choosing to become a professor, about moving to the middle of the country and just as all these thoughts are rising to the apex of your consciousness, you turn a corner—and there they are—

MICHAEL: Cookies.

JANE: Cookies. That's right. And they're not just any cookies, are they?

MICHAEL: No, they're not. They're plentiful and large. Almost what you'd call homemade.

JANE: And in some cases they are homemade. And warm.

MICHAEL: They were. Some of them were warm.

JANE: And what does that say to you?

MICHAEL: That they—recently baked them, or—

JANE: No, no, scientist—on a metaphorical level.

MICHAEL: Oh. Let's see—warm cookies.

JANE: Yes, what does that say?

MICHAEL: That "we—take care." That "we—baked cookies and care about you."

JANE: Right, like mommy. Like mommy did.

MICHAEL: My mommy never baked cookies.

JANE: I'm speaking emblematically here. I'm talking about what they're trying to do to you.

MICHAEL: They're trying to extinguish my fear.

JANE: But more than that, your doubts. How can anyone who provides me with ample warm cookies be exploiting me?

MICHAEL: Wow, that is evil.

JANE: Of course it is.

MICHAEL: But there's another way of looking at it, isn't there?

JANE: Oh?

MICHAEL: Yes, like for instance; Maybe they're just being nice and wanted to give us cookies.

JANE: New to academia, are you?

MICHAEL: Sort of.

JANE: Well, there is no "just" anything.

MICHAEL: You're right. They're trying to kill me.

JANE: Now you're getting it. Welcome to the academy, Michael.

MICHAEL: Thank you, Jane. Hey, I didn't see you at the introduction thing.

JANE: Oh, I can't do that anymore. I just don't go in much for forced collegiality.

MICHAEL: "Man is essentially a solitary being."

JANE: Be careful. You'd be wise to erase gender specificity from your vocabulary while you're here, or you'll get sick of being corrected time and time again.

MICHAEL: I'm sorry, you're right. "Man—and broads—are essentially solitary beings."

(She laughs.)

MICHAEL: Something tells me you're not a chemist. What with your having a personality and all.

JANE: Can you guess?

MICHAEL: Poli Sci.

JANE: Why can't I ever be a mystery?

MICHAEL: You're much more mysterious than I am.

JANE: Not so sure actually.

MICHAEL: Why do you say that?

JANE: I remember your resume. They sent it around.

MICHAEL: They "sent it around?"

JANE: Common practice. For all the new hires. Harvard, right?

MICHAEL: Guilty.

JANE: Very impressive.

MICHAEL: But not mysterious.

JANE: I remember thinking so. There was a gap.

MICHAEL: A "gap"?

JANE: That's right. I'm an expert at resume date manipulation. I used to do it myself. There's a way of implementing the dash—between dates, to make it look like you were never out of work.

MICHAEL: "Implementing the dash?"

JANE: Yes, there's the straight dash, which denotes "From this time to this time," and then there's another kind of dash—the kind of dash I remember your resume having. It wasn't a straight dash. It was more squiggly, and there was an ellipsis after one of them.

MICHAEL: "Eagle eye" Jane, is that how you're known around here?

JANE: So what about it?

MICHAEL: What about what?

JANE: The gap.

MICHAEL: I don't know if I'd call it a "gap."

JANE: What would you call it?

MICHAEL: A chronologic chasm.

JANE: So what were you trying to hide? Prison time?

MICHAEL: No.

JANE: A marriage on a lark. She was Russian. There was a mob connection.

MICHAEL: I did do a little time—in the military.

JANE: Hmm. That's it?

MICHAEL: I'm afraid so.

JANE: So why not put that down? You were in the military. What's there to be ashamed of?

MICHAEL: Who said I was ashamed?

JANE: You're right.

MICHAEL: Though your putting it that way proves my point.

JANE: Which is?

MICHAEL: I said military. You implied "shame."

JANE: Okay, you're a little right.

MICHAEL: If I had been applying to say—an insurance firm—do you think that association would have been made so quickly?

JANE: Oh, I see. Liberal arts college. Anti-military.

MICHAEL: Not consciously, no.

JANE: Just—

MICHAEL: Endemically. At its core.

JANE: We're sounding a little defensive, aren't we?

MICHAEL: No more than we're sounding a little patronizing.

JANE: What branch?

MICHAEL: Navy.

JANE: Cool. Did you drive a ship?

MICHAEL: Ships aren't "driven."

JANE: Sorry. So what did you do?

MICHAEL: I was just an "admin" guy. Office stuff. So what do people do around here for fun?

JANE: You mean other than avoiding lines of inquiry?

MICHAEL: Is there a kind of social life here?

JANE: "Kind" of one, yeah.

MICHAEL: Well, can I —can I buy you a cup of coffee sometime?

JANE: I suppose.

MICHAEL: When?

JANE: Sometime .

(MICHAEL *turns and we're in a classroom where we see a young man writing on an unseen black board.*)

MICHAEL: I don't think so.

AHMAD: *(Stops writing, turns to him)* With all due respect. Professor, you're wrong.

(The young man goes back to writing on the board, almost manic)

MICHAEL: Ahmad, you're forgetting about the relative Pka's —

AHMAD: We're in acidic conditions—that's irrelevant. *(He writes a little more.)* See?

(MICHAEL stands, taken aback)

MICHAEL: Oh. Well, I stoop corrected. Sorry about that. Actually, that's fine, Ahmad, let's just call it a day. *(Turns to unseen class)* Class dismissed. Keep working on the corollaries. See you on Thursday.

(AHMAD picks up his book bag and starts out.)

MICHAEL: Ahmad, could you stay a minute?

(AHMAD turns.)

MICHAEL: I uhm—I'm afraid we have a little bit of a situation here.

AHMAD: Yes.

MICHAEL: You're way ahead of me.

AHMAD: I am a little concerned.

MICHAEL: I imagine you must be.

AHMAD: Is there any way we could resolve this problem?

MICHAEL: Well, that's what I'm wondering. The only thing is,—and I don't mean this to sound as self serving as it does, but, I'm the best you're going to get in these parts.

AHMAD: I'm very anxious to learn.

MICHAEL: I could tell you are. It's just a little shocking, you know, compared to the rest of the kids here.

AHMAD: Yes, I know. I live in a house with six other students. All day and night there's television and fornication. M T V and magazines and talk about "Jerry Springer" and "primo weed."

MICHAEL: Well, I'm sorry to hear that. Are you able to get any work done?

AHMAD: Mostly I stay in the library. Sometimes I sleep in a study room.

MICHAEL: Well, as far as this class goes, perhaps we could arrange for you to study online.

AHMAD: That would be fine. Though, I would like to study with someone brilliant.

MICHAEL: You mean unlike me.

AHMAD: If possible.

MICHAEL: Gee, if I weren't so secure, I'd be insulted. Are you here for the year?

AHMAD: Why do you ask?

MICHAEL: I'm just curious.

AHMAD: I've checked in, if that's what you mean.

MICHAEL: "Checked in"?

AHMAD: Yes, with your Homeland Security. I'm all clean.

MICHAEL: I have no doubt you're "clean," Ahmad, I just asked so I could map out a course of study. How long will you be with us?

AHMAD: The year.

MICHAEL: Good.

(AHMAD *starts to leave.*)

MICHAEL: How do you like it so far? Clouds Hill, I mean.

AHMAD: I'm not here for fun.

MICHAEL: I know, I was just making conversation.

AHMAD: The women I notice—they're rather like whores.

MICHAEL: Whoa, Ahmad.

AHMAD: I mean their clothes, the way they talk.

MICHAEL: Well, you might want to tone down the rhetoric a little there. Strangely, some women get a little prickly when you call them "whores."

AHMAD: But the way they dress.

MICHAEL: Well, some of them, yeah.

AHMAD: So "some" of them are whores?

MICHAEL: No, that's— You can't really say—you know, how a person dresses doesn't really—

AHMAD: But it's how they act. I hear them. In the house I live in. I hear their heads beating against the wall in a rhythmic fashion.

MICHAEL: Well, those are particular girls.

AHMAD: So those particular girls are whores?

MICHAEL: Well no—

AHMAD: I can even hear it when the men ejaculate into them.

MICHAEL: Well, that's—that's very—

AHMAD: And none of them are married.

MICHAEL: Well, that may be true.

AHMAD: So, what would *you* call them?

MICHAEL: Well, I would say they're young women engaged in a consensual activity.

AHMAD: Where I come from they would be called whores. (He starts to leave.)

MICHAEL: You know, Ahmad, don't forget to hang out a little bit. Make a little time for fun.

AHMAD: That's not what I'm here for.

MICHAEL: I see. Well, I'll work on the course. Until then, try to put up with my inadequacies, okay?

AHMAD: *(No hint of irony)* I'll try.

(MICHAEL *turns, he's standing in front of* JANE *on the bench outside.)*

JANE: Why wouldn't he call them that?

MICHAEL: But if *I* called them whores.

JANE: You'd be an asshole.

MICHAEL: Because of where I was born.

JANE: Right, but that's true with everything. If you were African American and called someone an "N" word—

MICHAEL: I'd be down with my homies.

JANE: Right, but being that you were born in— I'm guessing New Jersey?

MICHAEL: Guess again.

JANE: You'd be considered a racist.

MICHAEL: And you don't find any of this ridiculous?

JANE: You're not going "A-W-G" on me are you?

MICHAEL: "A-W-G?"

JANE: Angry White Guy?

MICHAEL: No, I'm not going "A-W-G" on you.

JANE: You were moving in that direction.

MICHAEL: Maybe I was being moved in that direction.

JANE: Here it comes.

MICHAEL: What?

JANE: You're going to start implying that things are no longer the way they used to be. The shores of your identity are being licked by the waves of inevitability.

MICHAEL: It just occurred to me how I might get an "A" in your class.

JANE: How is that?

MICHAEL: Agree with you.

JANE: Not true.

MICHAEL: Stand here and tell me you don't indoctrinate those porous little minds.

JANE: I don't indoctrinate. I present.

MICHAEL: Really.

JANE: I present a world view.

MICHAEL: Whose world view?

JANE: The world view I've come to understand.

MICHAEL: "Americans are bad, the rest of the world is good. We're imperialists, colonialists, genocidal psychopaths and the cause of the world's problems."

JANE: That's not what I teach. What you need to do is take a quick peak at the immigration flow chart and the census once every four years to see that you're a dinosaur. And worse than that, your ideas are antiquated. I know your type. You walk around with a haughty superiority born out of the new victim status you've conferred upon yourself.

(AHMAD *appears off to the side, holding a soccer ball as* JANE *continues.*)

JANE: Which of course is more than a little ironic, being that for so many years—the world was a victim of you. And now we have to sit around and listen to this neo-con whine day after—

(MICHAEL *sees* AHMAD.)

MICHAEL: Ahmad.

AHMAD: I hope I'm not interrupting.

MICHAEL: Uh, no...not at all.

AHMAD: *(Holding up the ball)* I was trying to "socialize." Like you suggested.

MICHAEL: Well, how did it go?

AHMAD: No one here plays football.

MICHAEL: Oh, do you know —

AHMAD: Yes, I tried to get into your Modern Political Theory course, but it was closed.

JANE: Oh, too bad.

(AHMAD *just stands there.*)

MICHAEL: So, uhm—would you like to join us?

AHMAD: Yes.

(AHMAD *sits on the ground.* MICHAEL *and* JANE *awkwardly do the same. More awkward silence*)

MICHAEL: So, Jane and I were just talking about—

AHMAD: —how the world is a "victim of you"?

MICHAEL: So it seems.

JANE: I don't know if it's worth dragging him into it. *(To* AHMAD*)* We shouldn't bore you with this stuff. I imagine Americans must always try to engage you in conversations about things you don't want to talk about—just because you're not from here.

AHMAD: I'm happy to talk about anything.

MICHAEL: How is your living situation working out? Is it getting any better?

AHMAD: A little, yes.

MICHAEL: Good.

JANE: What happened?

MICHAEL: Oh, Ahmad was just having some trouble with a couple room mates.

JANE: You're not rooming with some local rednecks are you?

AHMAD: "Red-necks?"

JANE: There's a tremendous fear of the "other" here.

AHMAD: I don't understand—"other"?

MICHAEL: It's a kind of —academic moniker.

AHMAD: Moniker?

JANE: Not exactly.

AHMAD: But isn't everyone "other" than someone else?

MICHAEL: You would think, yes, but apparently some people are more "other" than other people are.

AHMAD: What a strange idea.

MICHAEL: I think so.

AHMAD: I should apologize to you. Do you mind if I call you "Michael"?

MICHAEL: Of course not. Why apologize?

AHMAD: I was rude to you. I said things that—looking back, were blunt and not thought out.

MICHAEL: That's quite alright, Ahmad. There's no need. Have you gotten in touch with my professor friend in Chicago?

AHMAD: Yes. We've started emailing each other, and the assignments are highly challenging. I'm very appreciative.

MICHAEL: No problem. The least we could do is teach you things you don't already know. *(To* JANE*)* Ahmad is way past go on anything I could teach him.

JANE: I'm not surprised. *(To* AHMAD*)* You come from the cradle of civilization after all—where higher learning was practically invented.

AHMAD: Do I?

JANE: Of course you wouldn't know that from reading the main stream press here. Nothing but a bunch of terrorists.

AHMAD: Do you not like your country?

JANE: What? Well, yes. In a way. Although lately I have some pretty big problems with it.

AHMAD: I see. Have you been to my part of the world?

JANE: No, but I plan to.

AHMAD: It would be good for you to see the difference.

JANE: No doubt.

AHMAD: I think America is a wonderful country.

JANE: Really?

MICHAEL: Well, stick around academia for awhile, Ahmad, we'll drum that out of you.

AHMAD: No, I appreciate it here. The chance to study. The freedoms.

JANE: You mean "Freedoms" in quotes.

AHMAD: What "quotes"?

MICHAEL: Hey, how 'bout those Red Sox lately, huh?

AHMAD: You have the freedom to have contempt for your country. Isn't that what you all had recently? All the demonstrations, all the bad mouthing of your president?

JANE: Well, he picked a pretty big fight.

AHMAD: But isn't that your opinion?

JANE: My opinion based in fact.

AHMAD: You seem disappointed.

JANE: About what?

AHMAD: That I don't agree with you.

MICHAEL: You know, you do seem disappointed.

JANE: Don't be ridiculous. He could believe whatever he wants.

MICHAEL: Hey, what do you know. It *is* a free country.

AHMAD: Do you know about the Moriori?

JANE: From the Chathams?

AHMAD: Yes.

MICHAEL: Who are they?

AHMAD: They were a people—very much like your own, I think.

JANE: They were a tribe from the Pacific Rim— they were one of the first known, relatively modern people to formally renounce war, even going so far as to castrate many of their male infants in order to diminish their innate war like propensity.

MICHAEL: Ouch.

AHMAD: They were subsequently slaughtered by the Maori. They had no leaders, no strong state organization. Almost every one of them was killed

MICHAEL: And how are we like them exactly?

AHMAD: Well, perhaps a case could be made that your country is doing the same thing. Castrating yourselves.

JANE: Or, a case could be made that we're becoming a War State—pre-emptively engaging anyone who even vaguely threatens us.

AHMAD: But how do you explain your men? The softening of your men?

MICHAEL: Yeah, what about us? Even our country singers are pansies now. Have you heard country music lately? It's all about feelings and love and crap.

AHMAD: Your men are ridiculous here. They're just woman with pants on.

MICHAEL: Some of them are women with dresses on.

(AHMAD *laughs.*)

JANE: Well, isn't this cozy?

MICHAEL: Well, come on Jane, the kid has a point.

AHMAD: Where I come from, men perform a certain function—and women perform a certain function.

JANE: And there's an aspect of that I agree with.

MICHAEL: Why do Muslims get a pass?

JANE: What?

MICHAEL: It seems to me that if Catholics treated women the way Muslims did, women's groups would be even more down on the Catholic Church than they already are. But yet for some reason, Muslims get a pass. Why is that?

AHMAD: I don't understand.

MICHAEL: Come on, you get a pass.

JANE: What's your problem with Muslims?

MICHAEL: I don't have a problem.

AHMAD: Well, you sound like you do.

MICHAEL: I just have a theory about it.

JANE: Is it offensive?

MICHAEL: I'm sure to someone it is.

JANE: I'd be careful if I were you.

MICHAEL: There, see! That's just it. "Careful."
That's why people give Muslims a pass.

AHMAD: Why?

MICHAEL: Because people are scared.

JANE: Of what?

MICHAEL: Of Muslims. Not Muslims in general,
no offense to you of course, Ahmad, but the more
fanatical variety. People are terrified.

AHMAD: Why are they terrified?

MICHAEL: Because very few other groups, religions or
organizations routinely order death threats on people
that disagree with them. Piss off some gay people, it's
bad, but they usually won't put a price on your head.
Don't serve a black person at a Denny's—boycotts and
picket lines and rightly so, but you don't hear them
threatening to kill the children of the Denny's manager.
There is a difference.

JANE: "Simplistic" is too flattering a word.

AHMAD: He's not exactly wrong.

JANE: What?

AHMAD: He has a point.

MICHAEL: It's just an observation.

JANE: How could you listen to this?

AHMAD: I should go.

(AHMAD *gets up, holding the soccer ball again*)

AHMAD: Next time lets play football.

JANE: Why, when "pile on the Muslims" is so much more fun?

(AHMAD *smiles.*)

AHMAD: Have a good day.

(AHMAD *leaves.* JANE *turns to* MICHAEL.*)

JANE: Stick to chemistry. Geo-politics isn't your strong suit.

MICHAEL: I happen to think it's better to hang a lantern on things.

JANE: Even your own prejudices?

MICHAEL: Especially my own prejudices. Would you rather I keep mine sublimated like some people?

JANE: Meaning me?

MICHAEL: I always equate modern day liberals with Victorians. They're both so scared of the power of language, of saying and doing the wrong thing. Don't you ever think of anything inappropriate, Jane?

JANE: Of course I do.

MICHAEL: I'm thinking something highly inappropriate right now. Would you like to know what it is?

JANE: I'm going to leave now. (*She starts to leave.*)

MICHAEL: Hey, was this our coffee?

JANE: Yes, consider this was our coffee.

MICHAEL: So, what about moving on to dinner?

JANE: I'm not interested, thank you. I'm not attracted to you. Was that "inappropriate" enough for you?

(She turns and leaves. MICHAEL stands frozen as the lights come up on AHMAD, writing on the chalk board again. MICHAEL steps forward.)

AHMAD: I didn't go to high school.

MICHAEL: You're telling me you taught yourself?

AHMAD: No, I had an uncle who was a chemist. He didn't know he was, but he was. Where did you learn chemistry—in the navy?

MICHAEL: How did you—

AHMAD: I deduced it.

MICHAEL: How?

AHMAD: My uncle used to call me "monstrously intuitive."

MICHAEL: I would say so.

AHMAD: I used to watch your ships off our coast. All of us used to watch them. Sometimes moving, sometimes not—often times they would pass in a long row of grey and blue silver —like a mile long snake. The elders in the village used to wish them away with curses.

MICHAEL: You don't say.

AHMAD: Yes, my uncle used to laugh at the size of the biggest boats. "How large" he would say. Sometimes when a bully puffs out his chest, he only exposes more of himself to the slings and arrows of his adversary.

MICHAEL: Your uncle sounds like a very smart man.

AHMAD: He was.

MICHAEL: What about him? Was he formally trained?

AHMAD: I'd rather not answer anymore questions.

MICHAEL: I only ask—

AHMAD: —to know more about me.

MICHAEL: Just idle conversation, Ahmad.

AHMAD: Then I'd like to idly converse with you.

MICHAEL: Feel free.

AHMAD: What did you think of us?

MICHAEL: When?

AHMAD: When you would look through your spyglass at us, from your big ships?

MICHAEL: I couldn't say.

AHMAD: And you can't imagine?

MICHAEL: Imagine what?

AHMAD: How we looked. We must have looked tremendously small. Like small dots, ridiculous, yes?

MICHAEL: I suppose that depends on who was looking through the glass.

AHMAD: And with the call to prayer, our getting on our knees, ridiculous.

MICHAEL: Why would you think that?

AHMAD: Because of the way your sailors would laugh at us—when they came ashore.

MICHAEL: They were just kids in a place they knew nothing about.

AHMAD: So then why would your country send your sailors to a place they knew nothing about?

MICHAEL: Now *that* is a good question.

AHMAD: In the dark I used to sit on the beach—and I would imagine that I couldn't be seen by your super duper high powered spyglasses—and I would look out at your biggest ship—one of your carriers—with lights out in the distance. And I would raise my hand and pretend that I had a string tied to it—slowly, slowly, I would imagine that I were pulling the ship in—closer and closer to me, as though I were the one in control of it—instead of the other way around.

MICHAEL: We were once like you, ya know.

AHMAD: "We?"

MICHAEL: Yes, "we"—"us"—Americans. We used to be the ones spied on. When the British, with the largest and most powerful navy in the world used to look at us through their "super duper" spyglasses— the rabble, the little provincial monkeys jumping up and down on the wharf in Boston. And no doubt they made fun of us as well—our un-civilized ways. And so we too began our life living in the shadow of large ships. But then we forget that—and our enemies sometimes forget that about us.

AHMAD: Will you be having sex with Jane?

MICHAEL: I'm not sure that's any of your business.

AHMAD: I'm just curious about the ways of courtship, that's all.

MICHAEL: As am I.

AHMAD: I'll drop my paper in your box.

MICHAEL: That'll be fine. I'll look over it, then forward it to our friend in Chicago.

AHMAD: Alright. (*He turns, starts out.*)

MICHAEL: Have a good rest of the day, Ahmad.

(AHMAD *exits as lights come up on the bench, on the green.* JANE *stands near it with* AHMAD.)

JANE: I wanted to apologize.

AHMAD: Why?

JANE: There was a—I don't know, a disconnect? I felt like I was judging you. Michael and I were talking about you, over you, as though you weren't a human entity unto yourself, but rather, someone or some thing that we were fighting over.

AHMAD: I did not feel that way.

JANE: Well, I'm glad to hear that. I'm not usually so—I'm usually more articulate. The world situation. Perhaps it's difficult for you to understand what I'm talking about but—you may have noticed a lot of things are happening. There's a sea change going on—

AHMAD: I'm not sure I understand.

JANE: Of course you don't. I'm not making any sense. But don't you feel at the center of it?

AHMAD: The center of it?

JANE: Yes, I mean, what's happening? I truly feel as though the world is losing its mind. And I feel as though our country is the tip of the spear. I want you to know I'm not any kind of liberal whack job. I came up as straight arrow as the rest of them—that is, girls, women of my generation. I went through the whole gamut, believing, not believing, trusting in authority, then not trusting again, then having moments—even now, where I trust it again. Because part of me wants to. It's just that it's such a small world. This one I mean. The world of the college. I was drawn to it because at least there's order and a modicum of politeness and propriety. I think that's why I like department meetings so much. It sounds insane, I know, but there's something about them—they're the opposite of the world. There's a beginning, a middle and an end—and it's clear where the end is. Because it says it, on the little agenda they hand out. "End here," it says. It's not as

though I couldn't make it in the outside world. At first
I felt that by coming here I was sort of—retreating.
But now I feel the opposite of that. How could people
say this isn't the real world? Have you ever worked
in the editorial offices of a foreign policy review
periodical? And *academia* isn't the real world? Or what
about Hollywood? I used to date a guy—what a joke.
He used to write things, you know, television scripts,
and he used to sit there and tell me that I wasn't in
the real world. Here at least people think. Try to dig
deeper—get at things.

AHMAD: The college makes you happy.

JANE: It does, yes. I even remember my first day as
an undergrad and the bolt of lightening that crashed
through me when I realized that people actually cared
about what I thought. I expressed myself more in that
first class then I did in seventeen years of sitting around
the dinner table with my family.

AHMAD: Are you rich?

JANE: Me? No. Why would you—I guess some people
could say I "come" from money, but it's not big money
or anything.

(AHMAD *moves toward her, picks a piece of lint off her
shoulder. She freezes.*)

JANE: Anyway, I just wanted to say I was sorry.

AHMAD: Why are you so nervous?

JANE: I'm not nervous. I'm just chatty. You should take
one of my classes—you'll see chatty.

AHMAD: Stand still.

JANE: What?

AHMAD: Stand still.

(AHMAD *moves toward her again. She moves away.*)

JANE: I'm sorry, I can't—this is—I just wanted to say I'm sorry and I am. I feel my own provinciality is reflective of my country's own provinciality and it makes me sick. I hate it. I can't tell you how much my country makes me sick. I'm ashamed of it. I'm sorry. I wish I could stand on a giant mountain and yell it to the rooftops that I am so sorry. For everything our stupid government does. It's not really us. None of it is representative of us.

AHMAD: Who is "us"?

JANE: You know—the ones who are thinking.

AHMAD: You mean here—at the college?

JANE: Here at the college, in the country where people think, anywhere.

(AHMAD *moves toward her again, but she moves away.*)

JANE: I'm sorry. I'm so sorry if it seemed as though— if you thought my asking you here—I take full responsibility for this. I'm not one of those hysterical little idiots who cries wolf, I just—I really did just want to tell you how sorry I am. I didn't mean to...it's not you, it's me. I'm sorry I asked you here. I must have given you the impression.

AHMAD: Perhaps it is I who should apologize.

JANE: Not at all. It's I. I mean me. I just. I probably put something out there. I just don't know what I'm sending. What to read. But tell me about other things. How are classes? How's the online class?

AHMAD: How well do you know Michael?

JANE: Not well at all. He's brand new, you know. Why, is everything okay?

AHMAD: Is he a full time teacher?

JANE: You mean, tenure track?

AHMAD: Yes. Is teaching all he does?

JANE: Are you asking me if he moonlights?

AHMAD: Yes, does he have another job?

JANE: Not that I know of. But if you feel he's not present enough for you there are steps you can take.

AHMAD: Steps?

JANE: Yes, you have options. You can write a letter to the dean.

AHMAD: No, I think he's doing the best he can.

JANE: But he doesn't challenge you. He does seem aware of that.

AHMAD: He just seems to ask me so many questions with two meanings.

JANE: Two meanings?

AHMAD: Yes, as though—there is the question he asks. And then there is the intent. Am I not saying it right?

JANE: No, no, that's fine. I'm just trying to get what you're getting at.

AHMAD: I wonder I suppose, if all he is—is a professor. He was in the military at one time, was he not?

JANE: Oh. You mean—oh.

AHMAD: Perhaps it's because I'm new to the country. I'm seeing skeletons in all the corners of the room.

JANE: No. No I think I know what you mean. He's so evasive. And it is—huh—it is funny.

AHMAD: Why do you think he's so concerned with my status?

JANE: What status?

AHMAD: As a student—staying here.

JANE: You mean your right to be staying here, to study here?

AHMAD: Yes.

JANE: I don't know. He has no say in anything like that. Why, did he give you the impression he did?

AHMAD: No, but I just wanted to state it—for the record—the concerns I have about him, to an independent person.

JANE: As in me?

AHMAD: Yes, in case something happened.

JANE: Like what?

AHMAD: I had a cousin in Michigan. He was deported.

JANE: When?

AHMAD: After the last attacks.

JANE: You're kidding me.

AHMAD: No, he had not filed for something.

JANE: Paperwork?

AHMAD: Yes, immigration.

JANE: What a travesty. I'm sorry about that. But you don't have to worry.

AHMAD: I don't want to bother you.

JANE: You're not. Not at all. I'm glad you told me this. I take it very seriously.

(AHMAD *gently takes her hand, sweetly kisses it.*)

AHMAD: Thank you.

(AHMAD *walks off as lights come up revealing* MICHAEL, *in a classroom.* JANE *is across from him.*)

JANE: We've gotten off on the wrong foot.

MICHAEL: It's my fault. I should just shut up when it comes to politics. I don't really know what I'm talking about.

JANE: That's not true.

MICHAEL: Well, I am sorry.

JANE: Wait, you're being sincere.

MICHAEL: I do sincere. I can do sincere and I can do flippant. *(Points to face)* This is sincere.

JANE: Why can't you be serious?

MICHAEL: Because it embarrasses me.

JANE: How is Ahmad doing?

MICHAEL: In what way?

JANE: How does he seem to you? Is he getting along?

MICHAEL: He seems fine. The guy up in Chicago I have him working with is up to his speed. He's falling asleep less in my class now, which I take as a great compliment.

JANE: What's your deal, Michael?

MICHAEL: What?

JANE: Who are you?

MICHAEL: Do you mean "who am I," as in "who are any of us, really?"

JANE: I don't know anything about you.

MICHAEL: Well, it's not like I haven't tried to remedy that.

JANE: Why are you questioning Ahmad about his status here?

MICHAEL: I'm sorry?

JANE: Why do you ask so many questions?

MICHAEL: Are you his lawyer?

JANE: I'm just wondering out loud, that's all. It's a different world nowadays, wouldn't you agree?

MICHAEL: You'll have to be more clear.

JANE: Since all of this has gone down, all the recent occurrences.

MICHAEL: "Occurrences" meaning—

JANE: Our interventions. Our increasingly global outreach. The purges here at home.

MICHAEL: The "purges"?

JANE: The draconian laws, the scaling back of our rights.

MICHAEL: Oh right, those.

JANE: I just think he's feeling a little pressure from that.

MICHAEL: Oh, Ahmad is feeling a little pressure?

JANE: And you—maybe you're just going into places you shouldn't.

MICHAEL: Is this what they mean by The New McCarthyism?

JANE: I don't mean to insult you, I really don't.

MICHAEL: Well then mind your own God damned business, Jane.

JANE: I consider that to have been an insult directed toward me.

MICHAEL: I meant that to be an insult directed toward you.

JANE: Now I would describe myself as uncomfortable.

MICHAEL: Well that's a startling coincidence, Jane, because I meant that to make you uncomfortable. You see if you would just step out of your *virtual* self and allow your *actual* self to be effected by what other people—in this case me—are trying to convey to you—you would experience the state that most people refer to as; "being alive."

JANE: Who are you to condescend to me?

MICHAEL: Strange, isn't it? Having someone disagree with you? Not like the classroom at all, is it?

JANE: I will not stand here—

MICHAEL: Shut up, Jane.

JANE: What?

MICHAEL: I said shut up.

JANE: You can say whatever you want to me—

MICHAEL: I just did.

JANE: STOP HARRASSING AHMAD!

MICHAEL: Ahmad is not being harassed. Believe me. It's not like he's a Jew in France or anything.

JANE: Stop it!

MICHAEL: Trust me when I say this Jane—you don't know one sixteenth of what you're talking about.

JANE: Who—*are*—you?

(*Blackout*)

END OF ACT ONE

ACT TWO

(In the dark, the same cello music from before. Lights up as we see MICHAEL *and* JANE *standing across from each other, a second later.)*

MICHAEL: "Who am I," Jane? Trust me when I say this: it will only *seem* as though I'm not answering your question.

JANE: And I'm "only as real as your perception of me." Is that it?

MICHAEL: Nothing is quite as diabolical as you think.

JANE: Why don't you let me be the judge of that?

MICHAEL: I have a colleague. A former colleague I guess you could say. He's in Chicago.

JANE: The "guy" in Chicago? The online guy?

MICHAEL: That's right. And I referred Ahmad to him—as you know, because I'm—deficient.

JANE: So...

MICHAEL: So he fills me in on how Ahmad is doing and he brought something up—just a little mention of something. And it piqued my—well not even my interest. It just made me think a little.

JANE: About what?

MICHAEL *(Referring to black board)* The work Ahmad has been doing. What it involves. When taken separately, it doesn't amount to much, but when you notice the pattern, he seems to be getting into things that could cause—concern.

JANE: Concern about what?

MICHAEL: Well, about what he may or may not be working on.

JANE: Well, what, drugs, or—

MICHAEL: —no, not drugs.

JANE: Tell me you're not implying what I think you are.

MICHAEL: It's just cause for curiosity, I'm not even saying concern.

JANE: Chemical weapons.

MICHAEL: There's what they call a precision balance—and it's missing—from my lab. Now the only reason someone would steal a scale like that—

JANE: —and naturally you thought the "kid from the middle east..."

MICHAEL: I haven't crossed any lines here, Jane, and this is not something I sought out. Now this friend of mine in Chicago, yes, he's a little "gung ho," —but my idea is to just try and contain it. He wants to raise a red flag, call someone on the—governmental level, and what I'm trying to do is prevent that. Because if someone does come snooping around, Ahmad is going to be deported or put in jail. Believe me, I worked around these people and they have people to answer to who have people to answer to and all Ahmad is going to be is a number. I'm not asking you to do anything, or go against any belief you have—but I do need for you to know that I'm not on the wrong side of this thing. It's my fault, I know, for even involving this Chicago guy because I agree with you; It is ridiculous and insulting and ugly and we can either ignore it, and Ahmad is going to be at great risk—or we could just clear it up here, right here on this little campus and no-one will be the wiser.

JANE: Why should I trust you?

MICHAEL: Because you don't have to.

JANE: Does this have anything to do with the "gap?"

MICHAEL: The "gap?"

JANE: In your resume. Your C V.

MICHAEL: I did a little time at—"X-Ray."

JANE: Guantanomo?

MICHAEL: Right. I did some administrative work down there.

JANE: Is that code for interrogate?

MICHAEL: I was a note taker. These weren't thugs from the neighborhood, Jane. These guys were Soldiers of God, straight up Al Queda. When they looked at you, it was like they were taking your picture in their head forever and you had a feeling that if they got out, they'd find a way to come at you. Or your family. Or your third frigging cousin. They had the restraints on, but it was *us* who felt vulnerable in the room.

JANE: And your friend?

MICHAEL: He was down there with me. He was the one asking about bio stuff. And we had one guy, one of the Al-Qaeda guys who ended up killing himself. Or so the report said. We were—around that.

JANE: How does a prisoner so heavily guarded— kill himself?

MICHAEL: Well, that's where—to tell you the truth— that's where I got a little confused as well. So I questioned it. And I was encouraged to take a little time off. What that meant was, they wanted me to resign my commission. And I did. And they were more than happy to see me go, Jane, which should give you a little more reason to trust me. It seems my questioning the way things were done down there, made me a little bit of a security risk.

JANE: What would you want me to do?

MICHAEL: Nothing, just—clearly Ahmad is enamored of you—

JANE: "Enamored?"

MICHAEL: You know—

JANE: And what, I'm supposed to do a Matahari on him?

MICHAEL: Just help him.

JANE: "Help him" how?

MICHAEL: By being truthful. By making him feel like he can talk to us. Open a up a window in him just enough so we could see there's nothing there.

JANE: You don't talk like someone who just "took notes."

MICHAEL: Or don't. Don't do anything. I'm just trying to help the kid, that's all.

JANE: But why me?

MICHAEL: Because, he doesn't trust me.

JANE: This feels unclean to me.

MICHAEL: The missing scale, Jane.

JANE: What?

MICHAEL: The scale. It's all that really matters.

(Lights diminish on MICHAEL, *up on* AHMAD, *near the bench. He and* JANE *stand across from one another.)*

AHMAD: Applications don't interest me. They never did. Applied science seems to me like working as a plumber.

JANE: Well, someone's got to fix the toilet.

AHMAD: Yes, of course, but I like understanding why it's broken in the first place. Or, what propensity exists within it that might lead to its proclivity to be backed up.

JANE: An idea guy.

AHMAD: Is that a bad thing?

JANE: Not at all. Were you encouraged when you were a little boy?

AHMAD: To do what?

JANE: Whatever you wanted.

AHMAD: Not at all. The ignorance around me was a blessing.

JANE: How could that be?

AHMAD: Because no one knew enough to discourage me.

JANE: And so it flowed out of you—like a savant.

AHMAD: I'm not sure what you mean.

JANE: I mean your talent. It just appeared.

AHMAD: It kissed me. I didn't kiss it. Is that what you mean?

JANE: Sort of. But why chemistry? That's what fascinates me about the different directions lives go. Why chemistry and not some other science?

AHMAD: You ask very inquiring questions.

JANE: Oh, I'm sorry, I'll stop. It's just-

AHMAD: —it's the very moment.

JANE: What "moment?"

AHMAD: In my mind's eye I imagine it deep in the
water, some sort of—I do not speak well enough to—

JANE: Of course you do, go on.

AHMAD: When I close my eyes I imagine trying to free
my mind from the perception of what we consider to
be—time.

JANE: Alright.

AHMAD: And when I do —when I'm successful at that,
it's easier for me to understand the idea of eleven
billion years of just—stillness—or one tiny section
of an infinite string—until that one moment, only four
billions years ago when something stuck together—
a confluence—a coincidence combining two or more
elements that ever so randomly happened upon a
combination that began—within literally, a micro
millisecond, four billion years of what we now consider
to be "life." Just a happenstance. A coming together
of two random bodies. And what if they never did?
We're only here now because of one floating chemical
happening to combine with another, but what if there
had been a wave that knocked into one of them or a rise
in the tide so that they never came together at all? If it
happened any later, we could still be crawling out of
the mud now with nothing but fish heads. And we
wouldn't be standing here on what someone randomly
decided to call a "college" on a lovely man made
constructed patch of green grass with coffee shops
and soda machines—everything imaginable that you
could dream of—from the pyramids to the Mayan
ruins to the skyscrapers to the baseball parks and the
flying jets to hot dog buns to the Spanish Inquisition
to Arnold Schwarzenegger.

JANE: Arnold Schwarzenegger?

AHMAD: Yes, Arnold Schwarzenegger. Even he is
nothing but the result of the random flow of tides—
spores, blown up through the atmosphere—with whole
worlds inside of them. And what, Professor Jane—
is the essential element of all that I have so inefficiently
described?

JANE: Like I would know?

AHMAD: Chemistry.

JANE: Chemistry.

AHMAD: Yes: "the properties of substances and the
transformations they undergo."

JANE: I see.

AHMAD: But it's the end. It's the end that fascinates me
even more.

JANE: The end of what?

AHMAD: Life.

JANE: What's so fascinating about it?

AHMAD: That no matter what, on some level, it'll be
nothing but a mirror image of the way it all began.
Where once there was an expanse, in the end, like the
last breath someone takes, there will be a contraction.
No matter how life ends on this earth; a nuclear
holocaust, an asteroid, the proximity of the sun,
whatever, there will be nothing but two distinct
chemicals again. During one microsecond they
will "be"—and only one microsecond later they
will "not be." And that—as they say in showbiz—
will be that. But I bore you.

JANE: On the contrary.

*(Awkward pause as he slowly approaches her.
She turns away.)*

JANE: How ridiculous.

AHMAD: What?

JANE: Oh, I was just—I realized—no, you'll laugh.

AHMAD: I will not laugh.

JANE: Okay, Michael...

AHMAD: Professor Michael?

JANE: Yes. He has this idea about you—

AHMAD: What about?

JANE: Oh my God, even thinking about it. I was going to—it's ridiculous, it really is.

AHMAD: What is ridiculous?

JANE: Well, he had this idea that you might—

(MICHAEL *suddenly appears.*)

MICHAEL: What, no football?

AHMAD: What?

MICHAEL: I thought next time we got together we were going to have a game of football?

AHMAD: Oh, yes.

MICHAEL: I hope I'm not interrupting.

JANE: No.

MICHAEL: I just came from the cafeteria. Has anyone tried the fried okra?

JANE: No I haven't.

AHMAD: What is okra?

MICHAEL: For the longest time I thought it was just another name for broccoli. Is it Jane?

JANE: What are you talking about?

MICHAEL: Okra. Is it just another name for Broccoli?

JANE: I don't—

AHMAD: Actually, I'm late for class.

MICHAEL: Don't let us keep you.

AHMAD: Yes. Have a good day.

(AHMAD *turns and leaves. Silence*)

JANE: Uhm—I don't uhm—I don't—

MICHAEL: Are you okay?

JANE: I don't feel comfortable with this.

MICHAEL: With what?

JANE: With doing what you asked of me.

MICHAEL: Well that's because you were right, Jane.
It was ridiculous not to trust Ahmad in the first place.
I'm a nutcase.

JANE: What do you mean?

MICHAEL: I mean your instincts are right. The whole
thing. "Guy from Chicago." It's ridiculous. I'm sorry
I even brought it up.

JANE: I couldn't be worse at it.

MICHAEL: At what?

JANE: Getting information.

MICHAEL: Oh please, don't even—Ahmad is a great kid.
I'll just handle my friend, everything will be fine.

JANE: "Fine"?

MICHAEL: Yes, it was all an over-reaction and I take
full responsibility. I even found the precision balance
thing—it was misplaced.

JANE: Was it?

MICHAEL: Yes.

JANE: I'm glad to hear that.

MICHAEL: No more glad than I am to say it. Trust me.

JANE: "Trust" you?

MICHAEL: Yes—I mean. If you want, trust me.
You don't have to.

JANE: I—don't.

MICHAEL: Sorry?

JANE: I don't trust you.

MICHAEL: I'm sorry to hear that.

JANE: How could it be a coincidence?

MICHAEL: What?

JANE: Your showing up. *(Pointing, where he entered)*
Just then.

MICHAEL: When?

JANE: When you would have thought you needed to.

MICHAEL: Oh, Jane.

JANE: I feel as though—even just being around you—

MICHAEL: Geez, Jane.

JANE: I think maybe I should talk to someone about this.

MICHAEL: About what?

JANE: I need to talk to someone.

MICHAEL: You're talking to someone now.

JANE: Ever since you've come here—

MICHAEL: Seriously, Jane. Are you alright?

JANE: Have you talked to anyone else?

MICHAEL: About what?

JANE: About what you talked to me about.
About Ahmad?

MICHAEL: No, but why—do you think I should?

JANE: I'm going to the Dean.

MICHAEL: To say what?

JANE: To document it.

MICHAEL: Document what?

JANE: What we talked about.

MICHAEL: Would she care?

JANE: Why wouldn't she?

MICHAEL: I'm not saying it's a bad idea. Maybe we should run it by her.

JANE: Now you're co-opting things. Everything I say, you....

MICHAEL: Jane, we could do whatever you want.

JANE: Stay away from me!

MICHAEL: Jane, I'm just—

JANE: STAY AWAY!

(JANE *runs out as the lights come up on* AHMAD, *seated in an apartment, reading aloud.*)

AHMAD: "Know of a certainty that no evil can happen to a good man either in life or after death. He and his are not neglected by the Gods. Nor has my own approaching end happened by mere chance."

(JANE *appears behind him. Barefoot. Shirt half open*)

JANE: I wish you hadn't seen my book collection.

AHMAD: It's the best way to get to know someone—without having to take them to dinner anyway.

JANE: It's important that you know—whatever I said during whatever we did—however I acted.

AHMAD: Is not who you really are.

JANE: That's the party line.

AHMAD: Or is it who you truly are—and this—this "professor" lady.

JANE: Careful...

AHMAD: Come to me.

(She walks over and they kiss.)

JANE: I am such—I can't believe-No, I'm not going to do talk. I don't do talk well. I just—just let it having happened, Jane—just—

(He kisses her again.)

AHMAD: When do you see the Dean?

JANE: Four.

AHMAD: I feel regretful about it. I don't want any harm to come to him.

JANE: Why? He doesn't seem to care too much about how you feel. He's arrogant. He's a—and it is bothersome, the more I think about it. He's just—so invasive—so out of bounds in so many ways. I'm sorry, but I think he's dangerous and I think my bringing this up is a service to you and a service to the rest of the students here and to myself as well. If he is who he says he is what's the harm? But if he's not, he's not worthy of this place. And the way he came on to me.

AHMAD: Did he?

JANE: Oh, please, like a boy. He's such a stupid simplistic boy. Most men his age are. They're all so searching and plodding and regretful.

AHMAD: And weak.

JANE: Yes, weak.

AHMAD: I miss my home.

JANE: I don't blame you.

AHMAD: No one here is close to themselves. Everyone is apart. Will they fire him?

(We see MICHAEL enter the classroom on the other side of the stage, ready for class.)

JANE: That depends. They may have to pay him for the rest of the year, but he doesn't have to work here.

AHMAD: I'm sorry. I'm still very sorry. He seems like a good man.

JANE: I better go. I'll be late.

(She kisses him. In the classroom, MICHAEL turns his head in the direction of JANE and AHMAD. He turns back to the blackboard.)

JANE: Will I see you tonight?

AHMAD: If you'd like.

JANE: I would like.

(AHMAD stares back at her as the lights fade, then come up again in the classroom. MICHAEL calls out to AHMAD before he leaves class.)

MICHAEL: Ahmad, is anything the matter?

AHMAD: Why do you ask?

MICHAEL: I mean I know I'm a knucklehead compared to you, and I know this class bores you silly, but I couldn't even get a smirk out of you today.

AHMAD: I apologize.

MICHAEL: Well, the work you're doing is amazing. Really, I never thought chemistry could read like a novel. Are you having fun?

AHMAD: I suppose.

MICHAEL: Well anyway—keep up the good work.

AHMAD: I'll try. *(He starts out.)*

MICHAEL: Oh, Ahmad— I'm asking everybody.
Have you used the lab on the second floor lately?

AHMAD: I'm not sure. Why?

MICHAEL: Nothing, there's just some misplaced scale
thing—a balance or something like that and the pencil
pushers were asking me about it.

AHMAD: I'm sorry, I didn't see it. I wish I could help
you.

MICHAEL: Oh, it's no big deal. They can't seem to keep
their records around here for crap.
You have a good night.

AHMAD: You too, Michael. *(He starts out, then turns back)*
Michael...

MICHAEL: What is it, Ahmad?

AHMAD: I just think—I think I should tell you—

MICHAEL: ...you know you can tell me anything,
Ahmad. There won't be any repercussions...for you.

AHMAD: I just wanted to say; I think you're an excellent
teacher.

*(MICHAEL looks disappointed he didn't hear what he wanted
to hear)*

MICHAEL: Thank you, Ahmad.

*(AHMAD exits as the lights slowly fade to black, coming up
on JANE. She is on the bench on the green. She is reading as
MICHAEL slowly walks up behind her.)*

MICHAEL: Déjà vu.

JANE: What?

MICHAEL: This is where we first met.

JANE: Oh. Yes.

MICHAEL: I uh—I just came from the Dean's.

JANE: I don't think it's appropriate we discuss this, actually.

MICHAEL: I'm just a little caught off guard, that's all. I would have thought you'd come to me first.

JANE: I don't think this is the appropriate forum to discuss this.

MICHAEL: This isn't a "forum," Jane, it's a bench, near a pond.

JANE: Regardless, this isn't the time or place.

MICHAEL: I came to say goodbye.

JANE: Oh?

MICHAEL: Yes. I'm not going to wait for their determination. I'm leaving today.

JANE: Well—part of me is sorry to hear that.

MICHAEL: Well, then "part" of me appreciates your saying that. *(He starts to leave, turns back.)*

MICHAEL: Jane, do you mind if I ask you just one question?

JANE: Don't you think you've asked enough?

MICHAEL: I understand your saying that, and I'm not raring up for a fight here, I promise—but I just wanted to know one thing.

JANE: What?

MICHAEL: How do you know?

JANE: What?

MICHAEL: That you're not wrong—about Ahmad.

JANE: Because I have knowledge. I have knowledge.

MICHAEL: Not a hunch?

JANE: No.

MICHAEL: Not a feeling?

JANE: No.

MICHAEL: And your becoming involved with him. You don't think that influences your perception at all?

JANE: What are you talking about?

MICHAEL: You're having sex with him. You don't think that taints your perception?

(She just stares back at him.)

MICHAEL: Okay, Jane.

(He starts to leave again. She then calls to him.)

JANE: Who the hell do you think you are?

MICHAEL: What?

JANE: What is it to you?

MICHAEL: You know what they say, Jane: "You can hear the grass grow around here."

JANE: I'm glad you're leaving. I'm glad I rid this place of you.

MICHAEL: Yes, it's a much safer place now, Jane, no doubt. *(He turns to leave.)*

JANE: How do *you* know?

(He turns back.)

MICHAEL: What?

JANE: That *you're* right?

MICHAEL: Because I have knowledge too.

JANE: Not a hunch?

MICHAEL: No Jane, not a "hunch."

JANE: And not a "feeling?"

MICHAEL: Not a feeling.

JANE: You don't even know him. That's what's so egregious. All this time and you've hardly gotten to know him. You weren't even smart enough to work with him. He's brilliant. You're nothing. You're jealous of his passion. And his beauty and his brains. You're a compromised soft failure. You don't know what he loves, what he dreams about, where he comes from. You don't know anything about him.

MICHAEL: On the contrary.

JANE: Why don't you ask your "friend in Chicago"— at least he could keep up with him.

MICHAEL: That would be hard, Jane.

JANE: Why is that?

MICHAEL: Because I am my friend in Chicago.

JANE: What?

MICHAEL: I am—my friend—in Chicago.

(She moves away.)

JANE: What are you talking about?

MICHAEL: He wasn't sending his work to Chicago— he was sending it directly to the office of one of our analysts. It's a very complicated world nowadays, Jane, many of us are going to have to be more than just one thing.

(AHMAD suddenly appears.)

AHMAD: Am I disturbing?

MICHAEL: Not at all. *(In flawless Arabic) Kana yajeb an tukhberani 'an-mizan. La anqadhana jamee'an. (Translation: You should have told me about the scale. It would have saved us all.)*

JANE: What is going on?

MICHAEL: Why shouldn't they come to a place like this, Jane? Where else would they find such a pliant clientele?

JANE: Ahmad, say something.

MICHAEL: Prisons and universities. That's where they'll sleep. Prisons and universities—two of the most discontented populations in the country. Where would you go? This is the place. This is the garden, Jane— nothing like a bunch of guilty white self loathing rich assholes to make them feel right at home. And you Jane, you're just a useful idiot.

JANE: *(Turns to* AHMAD*)* Ahmad, go!

MICHAEL: *(Quick, to* AHMAD*)* You're dealing with me now—you stay!

JANE: Ahmad!

*(*AHMAD *stays perfectly still, looking straight at* MICHAEL.*)*

MICHAEL: And you tell your brothers this;

*(*JANE *goes to cut him off.)*

JANE: GET AWAY FROM HIM!

*(*MICHAEL *expertly contorts her arm, pushes her aside.)*

MICHAEL: *(Staying on* AHMAD*)* If you hit us again, we will move in the night and we will kill you—

JANE: NO!

MICHAEL: NO ONE seeks vengeance like empire. You go back—AND YOU TELL THEM THAT!

(As JANE *screams—"NOOOOOO!"—loud cello music starts abruptly, as the lights bump dark.* JANE *stops screaming and the lights slowly come up again, accompanied by the sounds of the birds chirping once more. It's a couple*

days later as we reveal AHMAD, *standing, facing away from* JANE, *who is seated on the bench.)*

JANE: Have you seen the dogwood—by the pond?

(No response from AHMAD, *who remains perfectly still)*

JANE: Every year I find myself anticipating its blooming. Gorgeous. We don't appreciate what's around us enough. This is such a beautiful campus. And the lilacs. Oh. My mother came here before she died. She couldn't make out the horse statue and I kept telling her: "Mother, it's a horse." *(Mother's snooty voice)* "That is *not* a horse." "Yes mother, it is—it's rep-re-sen-ta-tion-al." Oh, she was too much.

(She looks at him. He doesn't move.)

JANE: He was insane. He was just a figment. They looked where he said he lived. There was nothing there. He was just a fraud. A madman. No one will ever know—the Dean couldn't be anymore discreet. It'll never leave the confines of this campus. And they'll waive your tuition. And they'll find you a house. Of your own. Of *our* own? It was just a nightmare, that's all. And when you wake from a nightmare— there's that delicious moment when you realize that that was all it was. And everything is just as it ought to be.

*(*AHMAD *turns, looks back at her, expressionless.* JANE *smiles, hopefully, never making eye contact with* AHMAD.)*

JANE: Just as it ought to be.

(As the lights fade slowly to black. And music comes up.)

END OF PLAY

"As the NDP foreign affairs critic at the time, I witnessed first-hand in Iraq the terrible impact of economic sanctions on the people of that devastated country. Mohammed Javed spoke out at the time with passion and dedication against these genocidal sanctions that killed over 500,000 innocent Iraqi children. He reminds us of this tragic history in this must-read book, which deserves a wide audience. We must learn the lessons of this dark chapter, and heed his powerful call to fight the rise of Islamophobia in Canada and beyond."

—Svend Robinson, former Member of Parliament from 1979 to 2004 for the New Democratic Party.

"Having written and spoken out about the devastating impact of sanctions on Iraqi children and people, I share Mohammed Javed's passion to ensure that we not forget and that we learn from this shameful event that we all witnessed, but only a few had the courage to call out. This book is a historic documentation of one man's passionate efforts to do his part to speak truth to power. We can all benefit from his perspective and insight on the issue and the lessons to be learned."

—Faisal Kutty, Lawyer, Law Professor, Writer and Public Speaker

"I am impressed by [the author's] commitment to justice and [his] efforts to promote it and to condemn the actions that caused so many deaths and suffering, particularly to children. [He] has put his heart and soul into writing this book."

—Mohammed Azhar Ali Khan, Retired journalist, civil servant and refugee judge, recipient of the Order of Canada and Order of Ontario.

"In the context of sanctity of human life and the universality of human dignity, Javed dedicates this book to "the memory of countless [Iraqi] children, [whose number could be as high as one million and], whose right to life has been usurped by cruel hands" during the first and second "Gulf Wars", the US occupation of Iraq and the series of US and UN wide sanctions.

As most of the world stood silently and helplessly, Javed, with the support of his family tried to "break the silence" through whatever modest means available to them. The author connects these man-made tragedies and the rising tide of evil Islamophobia and evil acts of terror that impacted the world at large.

Referring to the Qur'an (95:4-6), which deals with the innate goodness in the human soul, that is prone to be disregarded, he quotes the famous "convert" to Islam, Muhammad Assad who wrote "....On the other hand, man may retain, or regain, that original, individual perfection if he consciously realizes God's Oneness and submits to His laws."

The message to all is: "So, do good deeds, be good to others - don't hurt others, be good to the earth, be good to the world and create a better world for all to live in – for sure, good will go round and come back to you...", a fitting message for an enjoyable reading."

—Jamal Badawi, PhD, Professor Emeritus, Saint Mary's University, Halifax, NS, Canada

THE
BROKEN
SILENCE

MOHAMMED JAVED

 FriesenPress

Suite 300 - 990 Fort St
Victoria, BC, V8V 3K2
Canada

www.friesenpress.com

The Broken Silence:

*How we can and should speak up against the injustices
in the Muslim world and beyond*

Written By: Mohammed Javed

Editors:
Lubna Javed
Shamsia Quraishi
Bassam Javed

"O you who have believed, be persistently standing firm in justice, witnesses for Allah, even if it be against yourselves or parents and relatives. Whether one is rich or poor, Allah is more worthy of both. So, follow not [personal] inclination, lest you not be just. And if you distort [your testimony] or refuse [to give it], then indeed Allah is ever, with what you do, Acquainted."

– The Holy Qur'an 4:135

FOREWORD

The Holy Qur'an (95: 4–6) emphatically states: "Surely, We created man in the best structure and afterwards, We reduced him to the lowest of low: with the exception of those who have faith and do good deeds." Human life has been created in the best of mould, the best of form, and the best of nature giving the humans will and discretion and if they use these faculties wrongly, they are abased to be the lowest of the low. Children who are born pure, innocent, and in the best of nature are devoid of being abase or cruel. Muhammad Assad writes in *Islam at the Crossroads*, "... On the other hand, man may retain, or regain, that original, individual perfection if he consciously realises God's Oneness and submits to His laws." So, do good deeds, be good to others – don't hurt others, be good to the earth, be good to the world and create a better world for all to live in – for sure, good will go round and come back to you.

This book is dedicated to the memory of countless children whose right to life has been usurped by cruel hands. Loss of innocent life has been happening since humans came into existence, continues to happen as humans are existent, and will continue as long as humans exist. However, it is still our basic responsibility to stop this as much as we can. This book is also a tribute to all those parents who have lost innocent children to cruel hands.

I am hereby touching upon part of the story of the genocide of Iraqi children (could be as high as a million children at the rate of 200 children per day) in the last decade of the last millennium and the first decade of 2000. The UN Security Council, at the behest of United States of America, decided to take all necessary measures to reverse the Iraqi invasion of Kuwait and ensure the complete disarmament of Iraq's weapons of mass destruction and imposition of a broad sanctions regime. The sanctions regime against Iraq was originally established by UN Security Council Resolution 687 in 1991. This resolution and other subsequent resolutions placed wholesale restrictions for exporting and importing commodities without sparing a thought to the bare minimum essential human needs. This cruel sanctions regime, in addition to the First Gulf War (January 1991), the Second Gulf War, and the occupation of Iraq (March 2003 to December 2011) have brought about the massive destruction of a thriving society. Sanctions commenced after President Bush Sr. waged the First Gulf War; President Clinton vigorously imposed the sanctions, followed by further mass destruction when President Bush Jr. invaded Iraq under the false pretext of weapons of mass destruction.

In fact, the sanctions regime is the real weapon of mass destruction and the sanctions themselves are 'Satanic Sanctions' and the hands that initiated, implemented, and enforced these sanctions are 'Satanic Hands of Satanic Humans' that deprived innocent children of their right to live, play, and love and be loved.

This book deals with how I strove, in my humble capacity, to work on opposing the sanctions regime to persuade the Canadian government by utilizing the media and by working with a group called *Nova Scotia Campaign to End Iraq Sanctions*. Svend Robinson, a prominent NDP Member of Parliament, tirelessly persuaded the Canadian government to lift the sanctions. This book includes:

- Correspondence with Svend Robinson (Member of Parliament from 1979-2004 who now works for a global fund in a senior position in Geneva), Hon. Jean Chrétien, former Prime Minister of Canada, Lloyd Axworthy (former Foreign Affairs Minister), Art Eggleton (former Defence Minister), Bill Graham (former MP and Chair of the *Standing Committee* on *Foreign Affairs and International Trade*). I have included my comments on the correspondence.

- Hearings of SCFAIT, House of Commons Debates, House of Commons Report and Recommendation.
- Humanitarian flight proposal to Iraq.
- Reproductions of some of my published letters and articles about Iraq sanctions (from *Chronicle Herald, Mail Star* of Halifax, and *Daily News* of Halifax).
- My correspondence (from 2013 and 2014) with Svend Robinson. He has furnished me with his speech at Baghdad Conference held on 7th May 2002.

The final chapter is about the current quagmire in the Middle East, specifically its impact on North America, including the rising tide of Islamophobia. The First Gulf War of 1991, the Iraq sanctions, followed by the Second Gulf War in Iraq and other American wars in the Middle East have given rise to terrorism in the Middle East and across the world, leading to the rise of Islamophobia. What goes around comes around and, for sure, we are witnessing the consequences here in North America.

In April 2013, I had a chance to meet the Honourable Justin Trudeau, then leader of the Liberal Party of Canada. I was able to ask him a question about Islamophobia: "When criminals commit an act of violence or terror, and if such an act is committed by a Muslim, the media loves to get into a 'hyperactive' mode and indulges in a hate campaign blaming Islam, which is a false notion and contrary to what Islam teaches and promotes. Such hate campaigns are not at all conducive and they certainly promote hatred of Islam, including hate crimes. In the public interest, I feel there is a need for some legislation to control the media from fomenting such hatred. Would your party look into promoting such legislation?" Justin gave a fairly elaborate response and said that, "I would prefer that it stay in the public sphere rather than in private conversation because then we can deal with the misunderstanding as a community. We have to work together because that's what Canada is about."

In the last chapter, I have dealt with Islamophobic incidents, its causes, statistics, and predictions. Then we have the remedies that are being worked out to curb Islamophobia in Canada, such as passing of anti-Islamophobia motions in the Canadian Parliament and Ontario Legislature. This chapter also covers an important aspect that we, Muslims, have to readjust our priorities and then more essentially, correct ourselves by following the *Sunnah*, the tradition of the holy Prophet Muhammad (peace be upon him) who is the best guide, a blessing to the universe and who taught the Divine Code of Conduct as revealed in the Holy Qur'an.

A book like this, I am sure, is the need of the hour and invaluable in dealing with the rise of both terrorism and Islamophobia in order to make our country safe.

INTRODUCTION
IS THERE A CORRELATION BETWEEN SANCTIONS AND THE RISE OF TERRORISM?

This originally appeared as an article on Huffington Post Canada on 10 April, 2017 and was written by my daughter, Lubna Javed.

The UN Security Council imposed stringent economic sanctions on Iraq on 6th August, 1990, four days after the Iraqi invasion of Kuwait. When the first Persian Gulf War had succeeded to oust Iraq from Kuwait the following year, the Security Council did not proceed to lift all the sanctions. Passed in April 1991, after the war, UN resolution 687 required Iraq to disclose and destroy its nuclear, chemical and biological weapons and to refrain from developing others, and called for war reparations to Kuwait.[1] The sanctions stayed in effect until May 2003. They banned all trade and financial resources except for "medicine and health supplies" and "in humanitarian circumstances" foodstuffs, the import of which into Iraq was tightly regulated.

The sanctions had a harsh impact on Iraqi civilians. By 1999, UN figures estimated that more than 1.7 million Iraqi civilians had died as a result of the sanctions, between 500,000 and 600,000 of whom were children. These numbers are disputed; however, even the conservative estimates are dismaying. Former assistant secretary general of the United Nations, Dennis Halliday, quit in protest in 1998 after one year as the UN humanitarian coordinator in Iraq. He described the sanctions as genocidal.

Dr. Richard Garfield, a professor at Columbia University noted, "Prior to the Gulf war, an estimated 97 per cent of the urban and 78 per cent of the rural population had effective access to curative services. By 1997, the capacity of the curative health system was greatly reduced ... the number of reported operations dropped by 70 per cent nationally, the number of laboratory tests performed dropped by 60 per cent, an estimated 30 per cent of hospital beds were no longer in use, about 75 per cent of all hospital equipment no longer worked, and a quarter of the country's 1305 health centers closed. A reported 80 per cent of all medical equipment was out of service."[2]

Sanctions led to the deterioration of what was previously an excellent national health service.[3] Thousands of Iraqis died of malnutrition, infectious diseases, and the effects of shortages or unavailability of essential drugs. Doctors suffered from intellectual embargo and found it difficult to obtain medical books. They were unable to travel aboard to attend medical conferences or training courses. Donations of medical books and journals by foreign doctors made to Iraqi medical schools and medical associations never reached the intended recipients.

A Canadian MP, Svend Robinson, moved to have the sanctions lifted in the House of Commons in May 2001, "The sanctions certainly have not had an impact on Saddam Hussein, but over the course of the last decade, they have resulted in the death, according to UNICEF, of over half a million children under the age of five ... What our delegation witnessed on our return last year was the total collapse of Iraq's human and physical infrastructure, a nation that has experienced a shift from, as was described by the United Nations development program, relative affluence to massive poverty. Unemployment is epidemic. Inflation has skyrocketed. The average salary is about $5

U.S. a month. There has been a dramatic increase in begging, prostitution and crime."[4]

The American and coalition forces invaded Iraq in 2003. The purpose of the invasion was "to disarm Iraq of weapons of mass destruction, to end Saddam Hussein's support for terrorism, and to free the Iraqi people."[5] Later, there were revelations that Saddam Hussein had no weapons of mass destruction. There was no concrete evidence discovered linking Hussein to terrorists. The removal of Saddam led to political instability and to the rise of sectarian insurgencies. The ensuing power struggle for the control of Iraq and ethnic division wreaked havoc on the country. Noam Chomsky, professor at the Massachusetts Institute of Technology states that ISIS "is one of the results of the United States hitting a very vulnerable society with a sledgehammer, which elicited sectarian conflicts that had not existed. It is hard to see how Iraq can even be held together at this point. It has been devastated by U.S. sanctions, the war, (and) the atrocities that followed from it."[6]

Lydia Wilson, journalist and research fellow at University of Oxford, interviewed ISIS prisoners in Iraq. She noted that young recruits were not attracted by religious fanaticism but because of how their families were treated under the U.S. occupation of Iraq and the repressive U.S.-backed government in Baghdad. They were ignorant about Islam and had difficulty answering questions about their faith. She wrote, "They are children of the occupation, many with missing fathers at crucial periods (through jail, death from execution, or fighting in the insurgency), filled with rage against America and their own government. They are not fuelled by the idea of an Islamic caliphate without borders; rather, ISIS is the first group since the crushed Al Qaeda to offer these humiliated and enraged young men a way to defend their dignity, family, and tribe. This is not radicalization to the ISIS way of life, but the promise of a way out of their insecure and undignified lives; the promise of living in pride as Iraqi Sunni Arabs, which is not just a religious identity but cultural, tribal, and land-based, too."[7] One of the prisoners interviewed stated, "The Americans came (and) they took away Saddam, but they also took away our security. I didn't like Saddam, we were starving then, but at least we didn't have war. When you came here, the civil war started."

There have been numerous studies done that examine the impact of sanctions on terrorism. One such study by Seung-Whan Choi and Shali Luo of University Illinois argues that "sanctions intensify economic hardships on the poor within countries and this increases their level of grievance and makes them more likely to support or engage in international terrorism. Economic sanctions are conceptualized as creating an opportunity for rogue leaders to manipulate aggrieved poor people to terrorize foreign entities who are demonized as engaging in a foreign encroachment on the sanctioned nation's sovereignty. Although the main purpose of economic sanctions is to coerce rogue countries to conform to international norms and laws, they can unintentionally produce a negative ramification and become a cause of international terrorism."[8]

In January 2017, President Donald Trump signed an executive order halting all refugee admissions and temporarily barring people from seven Muslim-majority countries: Iraq, Iran, Libya, Somalia, Sudan, Syria, and Yemen. It is interesting to note that the seven countries on which the Trump's government-imposed travel bans have had U.S. imposed sanctions on them.

CHAPTER 1
THE LETTER

*"O my son, establish prayer, enjoin what is right, forbid what
is wrong, and be patient over what befalls you. Indeed, [all] that is
of the matters [requiring] determination."*
—The Holy Qur'an 31:17

9 February, 1998

February 1998 was the time when the Iraq situation was getting tense
again. Saddam Hussain was still in power; the US was threatening to
use force as there was a dispute over allowing UN weapons inspectors into Iraq. Alexa McDonough, the leader of NDP, took a stand in
Parliament for a peaceful resolution to the Iraqi crisis.

The day of 9 February 1998 was a usual winter day including the
usual substantial snowfall when I was in the midst of my struggle
to re-establish here in Canada after migrating in January 1994. We
achieved the status as Canadian landed immigrants in June 1993 and
then returned back to Saudi Arabia for six months. We originate from
India; however my place of work was Saudi Arabia. At that time, in
Halifax, I did not have a professional job or even a job. I was in the
midst of a process to get out of the mess of selling my laundromat on
a promissory note, trying to get the promissory note money, trying
to chase the man who bought from me goods on the basis of false
post-dated cheques, hoping to do some courses and get my professional engineering licence and of course get a job. Obviously, it was

important for me to re-establish to sustain myself and my family consisting of my wife, Naheed and three children - daughter, Lubna aged 19, son, Hisham aged 14, and another son, Bassam aged 9 years at that time.

My wife supported me in my business ventures and also sent out my résumé to hundreds of prospective employers in the U.S and Canada. My wife and I used to share the work of dropping and picking up the children from their schools. Our sons' schools were close by but my daughter was attending a school in Halifax which was about 25 km from our home in Lower Sackville. On a good day it took about half an hour to drive to her school. Quite a few times she would keep me or her mother waiting in the car in those cold days when the temperature would drop to several degrees below zero. Of course she used to be apologetic about it and even now she acknowledges that she used to keep us waiting. She became a good engineer, graduating from Dalhousie University in Halifax. We have pleasant memories of her high school graduation day when she came out with flying colours receiving numerous awards; it was heart-warming and exciting to see Lubna Javed get on the stage numerous times to receive those awards. Later on, Hisham graduated from Carleton University in Ottawa in Information Technology and Bassam got his Master's degree in Engineering from University of Ottawa. Great! Thank you, Canada!

It would be worth mentioning at this point that my wife took care of all the household work so I was relieved of performing such duties; I was not allowed in the kitchen for cooking activities for obvious reasons – so it gave me time to pursue the sanctions activism.

Now let us have a look at the story and how the individual activism against Iraq sanctions began in a unique manner consisting of correspondence, first with the Prime Minister of Canada, and then with other Federal Ministers and other sympathetic MPs, especially Svend Robinson. The activism was reinforced by my letters to the editors of local Halifax newspapers. Those letters to the editors were blunt. Canada has and had freedom of expression. I used my freedom of expression for a great cause. Thank you, Canada! I was not worried about any repercussions for being so critical and even if there were any, I was prepared to face them for the sake of humanity, for the sake of dying Iraqi children. There were no repercussions in Canada or even in the U.S and I secured a good job as an engineer in California's Transportation Department and worked with them for six years from 2001–2007 to build the new San Francisco–Oakland Bay Bridge. Just before that I had worked for a year in a private engineering firm in Napa.

Right from the time we migrated to Canada, I used to get involved in community activities in Halifax-Dartmouth through the Islamic Association of Maritime Provinces (IAMP); I was the Secretary of the Association in 1996. As the Iraq situation was getting tense, we started to organize to act in our own lawful capacities to prevent the possible Gulf War II and pursue a peaceful resolution. Canada was a U.S ally in the first Gulf war and remained so.

I remember Dr. Jamal Badawi – Islamic scholar, leader and professor at Saint Mary's University, encouraged us to contact our MPs and to write to the Prime Minister as government policies are formed based on people's opinion and representation. It was also discussed if we could arrange to have a meeting with the Prime Minister wherein a few representatives could meet him and present a memorandum to desist from another war and resolve the matter in a peaceful manner.

Yes, then I wrote to the Prime Minster Jean Chrétien on 9 February 1998 and as I have indicated, it was a significant day for the story of sanctions - the story of my activism began on that day. I was sure that I would get a response, however, I did not think if it would have a positive impact or not, but I surely wanted to convey the important message of peace to the Prime Minster. I chose a nice blue-coloured sheet of paper for the letter that I mailed on the same day, and sent it through email too. Subsequently, I wrote to Alexa McDonough, the NDP MP and leader of the party thanking her for the stand that they took in Parliament.

At this point, it may not be out of place to talk about other related activism in Halifax – to hold a peace rally in the town. IAMP organized it, and I was part of the team. Many other organizations in the Halifax-Dartmouth area and student associations too joined the effort and the peace rally was held on 20 February 1998. About 300 people joined the rally and at the end of the march we gathered at Grand Parade in downtown Halifax. Dr. Jamal Badawi, keynote speaker in his speech gave the message of peace and said that use of military force will result in civilian deaths and will likely fail to unseat the Iraqi dictator.

Well, getting back to the letter I wrote to the Prime Minister, I got an email response on 20 March 1998 from L.A. Lavell, Executive Correspondence officer stating that the issue falls within the portfolio of the Honourable Lloyd Axworthy, Minister of Foreign Affairs and that he has taken the liberty of forwarding my email to the Minister that he too may be aware of my comments. This opened the way to further communicate with the minsters and MPs. By the way, I received a written response from Keith Hanash, Special Assistant – Correspondence, Office of the Prime Minister too. And the story of sanctions, and the activism too continued their march and the relevant happenings in the subsequent twenty years gave me enough material to write this book containing not only the impact of sanctions and war but its reaction too, including a look into the causes of Islamophobia. In the process I had an opportunity to reflect into my personal life and how my life incidents moulded me.

CHAPTER 2
GROWING UP IN INDIA

"And that there is not for man except that [good] for which he strives."
—The Holy Qur'an 53:39

13 December, 2017

Yesterday, we (Naheed, Lubna and I) went on a hike in Pleasanton (East Bay area of San Francisco). It reminded me of a childhood story when I was about seven years old. The valleys and ridges covered with grass is a characteristic of the Bay Area and when it is green it is beautiful. Now it is half green and half dried up – the hiking area was covered with different types of oak trees and even olive trees. It was a beautiful sunny day with temperature in the morning at 0°C and then rising to 18°C at about 1.30 p.m. Tagged cows were grazing and at a point we saw a few cows who seemed to have a sumptuous meal of grass and were resting in the abundant shade of oak trees. Some of them started staring at us and continued to do so by turning their heads – that was strange, perhaps, they were looking at the 'human animals' who are different from them. I was asked to lead the way for obvious reasons. I take my hiking stick, which helps me when terrains are difficult and it is a protection from possible encounters with wild animals including unleashed dogs – of course dogs are generally well trained on trails but when they come too close to us I firmly say "No" and then apologize to the dog owners for staying away from them and of course I do praise by saying: "You have a beautiful dog!" We hiked for two hours taking 7000 steps and covering a distance of 4 km - with somewhat high slopes though gradual.

Anyway, here is the childhood story: I was on my red-coloured tricycle, riding it on a sidewalk outside the house in Madras (Chennai now). Cows on the sidewalks were common in those days. A cow charged at me with her head bowed towards me. A relative uncle of mine known as *Dada* who owned a vegetable shop right there, came to my rescue with a *'danda'* in his hand, and I was not hurt. I might have cried but learned that cows do not like the colour red! Our hiking team did not wear any red or very brightly coloured garments now but it remains a surprise why the cows stared at us!

But not all stories worth remembering involved being attacked by wayward bovines. Two tender incidents with my sister come to mind. I think, I was about six and a half years old, and it was summer. My sister is more than two and a half years younger than me. We were in our nani's (maternal grandmother) house, visiting Hyderabad from Madras. The layout of the house was such that it had a large sit out verandah in the rear portion of the house without any wall on the side that opened in the backyard. The floor was about six feet high without any railings at the edge and was connected with steps to the ground and adjoining those steps, there were trees and bushes and one of those was a papaya tree. My sister was unknowingly moving back and would have fallen six feet below to the ground had I not rushed and grabbed her preventing her potential fall! I still remember my Dad, Mom, aunts, and others commending my timely compassionate and considerate act!

I think again, I was about six and half years old and it was summer when we were visiting Hyderabad from Madras. My Dad took us for a short joy ride in a small plane (4-seater). It was exciting but scary too! My same sister was seated next to me, and I think when the flight got little bumpy, I extended my hand and held her arm tightly, acting as an elder brother to potentially protect her from the perceived danger of falling down. Again, I remember well that my Dad and Mom praised me!

Looking back and reflecting on those two incidents I think that the compassion and care that was evident in my childhood days continued in later life and fits in with my action to participate in individual and group effort to lift the Iraq sanctions!

CHAPTER 3
A NEW IMMIGRANT'S TALE

"But verily thy Lord – to those who leave their homes after trials and persecutions, – and who thereafter strive and fight for the faith and patiently persevere – Thy Lord, after all this is oft-forgiving, Most Merciful."
—The Holy Qur'an 16:110

23 May, 1998

Rather than a single event, I would say, a chain of events including the circumstances and their outcomes have profoundly affected my personal as well as professional life in Canada since we migrated in January 1994. Though the outcomes of events would appear to be a failure, I would not term them so. In fact, I have emerged stronger after each event. The trials of destiny have made me know myself in more depth, put me on track of knowledge and have brought me to the doorsteps of University College of Denver.

A chain with its links connects a post or a pillar with another before beginning to run again. Similarly, there are posts or pillars or milestones in every life interlinked with a chain of events. Here the story begins with the milestone of coming to Canada and moves to the second one that knocks at the doorstep of knowledge.

When we came to Canada, I had to resign my job. I had to quit after more than 17 years of service as a civil engineer, a project engineer in a power company in Saudi Arabia. I had practiced for a total of 24 years as a civil engineer, specializing in construction and project management. We were prompted to do so to seek North American education for our three children and also partly because of my wife's desire. In addition to these factors, I also had in my mind the stagnation in life that to a substantial extent was created by my employer in their quest for 'Saudiazation'. However, when I had begun the process of resignation, my project manager, knowing my work capabilities, honesty, and dedication, tried his best to retain me and also fitted me in the slot of a senior project engineer.

Canada, as a pre-condition of immigration, wanted me to be an entrepreneur, and I did it by venturing into the import field and brought a fairly significant quantity of goods from India. The man who prompted us to import became our distributor. The outflow of goods was substantial but soon we realized that the inflow of money was not at all matching. Thereby, we were left alone to move on our own distributing and marketing in all the Maritime provinces. We did manage to sell the goods but still a substantial quantity of a certain product was left unsold as of May 1998 as the manufacturer shipped the wrong colour. This happened in spite of quality control by a person well known to us. Another commodity was also left unsold due to overstocking. And this happened due to cancellation of an order that we placed being delayed. We placed a similar order from another manufacturer. But finally, both shipments arrived.

In another venture, I signed a recruitment agency agreement with a Saudi employment firm. We did succeed in sending a few candidates for employment to Saudi Arabia but ended up in financial loss as the Saudis' were keener on hiring than those who were being hired. In one case, a candidate after accepting an offer declined saying that his girlfriend would not let him go.

Another venture was the export of wooden poles to Saudi Arabia. In Saudi Arabia, I was appointed as an agent to represent a major Canadian wooden pole producing company. But the Canadian poles with slightly lower fibre strength were not successful.

I bought a large juice dispensing machine, trusting a salesperson that misled me with wrong sales figures. I bought a laundromat business, washed the dirty linen, hardly made minimum wage and returns despite investment of a substantial value.

I continued with the sale of commodities imported. I sold a few thousand dollars of goods to a person on post-dated cheques. All the cheques bounced. The Royal Canadian Mounted Police would not lay fraud charges, as I implied, by accepting post-dated cheques, that a loan was acceptable to me. The RCMP therefore would not dare to charge as they would not be able to prove intent to commit a crime. I made a hue and cry, got attention from the media and made news because "the importer was in bind by accepting post-dated cheques." I pointed out the weakness of Canadian law pertaining to business transactions.

I subsequently won the judgement but not the money. I wrote to the provincial Minister of Justice without any success, however, it made the news titled, "Importer Burned by Bad Cheques". I wrote to the federal Minister of Justice where the weakness of Criminal Code was acknowledged by the provincial Ministry of Justice officials. The Minister of Justice and Attorney General for Canada wrote back, "As you know, the provinces are responsible for the criminal prosecution of fraud cases in the provinces. To date, none of the provincial attorneys general have asked the article 380 of the Criminal Code be amended and, at present, I have no plans to introduce such changes. I agree with the Honourable Jay Abbas, Minister of Justice of Nova Scotia, who wrote to you that the present laws are adequate. However, I will bring your concerns to my officials for their information." This did not surprise me because I was told that in Canada, if my dog bites a thief who is in the process of stealing, he can sue me for damages caused by the dog's bite. Therefore, I dropped the idea of having a dog and also because my youngest son is scared of dogs and my wife does not like them. Do you think she too is scared of dogs?

I sold the laundromat in 1996 with some down payment but a major portion was left to be received on a promissory note. I went to Saudi Arabia, represented a Canadian power company that was willing to export their technical services to another power company in Saudi Arabia. This time, the Saudi Arabian side was keener but the Canadian side did not take much interest probably due to lack of their own resources.

In the meantime, when the above ventures were in progress, I was also preparing for three technical examinations required for me to get admitted to APENS (Association of Professional Engineers of Nova Scotia). Probably, my bachelor's degree appeared to them as having been obtained from the land of apes; however, it did help me in enhancing my knowledge. And I used the highway engineering knowledge to pursue and then organize a petition of residents to eliminate the sound pollution of zooming vehicles penetrating the window of our bedroom especially on the weekend nights.

I was enrolled only as an engineer in training in February 1996. Before I received my professional engineer status I would require passing a professional practice exam and a year of Canadian work experience (all the experience in the world was not sufficient for them).

I searched for professional jobs in Halifax and even voluntary jobs so that I could obtain my one year of Canadian experience. Halifax did not yield results. By this time, I was getting financially drained and problems started brewing on the promissory note repayment from day one. When we demanded the first installment of repayment of the promissory note, the man shot back, "Which money?" We wondered if it was due to loss of some memory!

I started trying for jobs assiduously on the Internet (of course anywhere in the world including the USA). I filed a lawsuit to get the payment on the promissory note and followed up vigorously going through a three-hour cross examination by the defendant. Any minute element of the word promissory note that could at least be visible with an electron microscope was not evident. Then we won a judgement in November 1997 but were not fortunate enough to win the lottery of payment.

I did some computer programming courses in Halifax, and a thought developed that programming could give solutions to construction and project management problems. With my newly-achieved programming knowledge, I went to Denver and consulted a career management company. I hired their services, got back to Halifax and tried vigorously, using the techniques that I learnt, to follow up with 'Thank you' letters in the process of building rapport with employers. I received some nice responses from the Presidents and Vice Presidents of multibillion, multinational firms that they had carefully looked into my résumé and that it was impressive; but unfortunately, there were no suitable vacancies now, however they would keep it on file for six months and get back to me as and when the need arises.

As I was in that part of a land where I probably looked alien to employers, I wanted to move to Toronto or Denver to look for a job but in the meantime a job offer was communicated to me from my previous employer in Saudi Arabia. Somehow, they refused. I used career management techniques and they were impressed, so I almost secured the job but then they said they would hire me only on an Indian passport and not on a Canadian passport. The process took about seven months including travels to LA as DHL was kind enough to lose my application package. On my way back, I stopped in New York to authenticate my degree but the Indian Embassy would not do so without seeing my Indian passport. I went back to Halifax and travelled again to New York and got the degree authenticated. But now, the Canadian Foreign Affairs Department would not accept New York's authentication. To expedite and sort out things, I went to Toronto and Ottawa and got the authentication done. When my previous employer refused to hire me on a Canadian passport they promised to hire me through a consultant or a contractor but it was easy for them to break their promises.

Finally, I went to Denver using a previously purchased ticket and learnt that the chances of getting hired by my old employer were ruled out. I woke up in beautiful Denver with a strong determination and inclination to pursue my computer studies. I discussed this and learnt that Denver would be able to offer the courses I was looking for – a Master's degree program in computer information systems.

So here I am at the next milestone ready to strive in pursuit of knowledge. Though I was financially broke, my spirit, determination and the urge strengthened in the process. As far as our financial needs were concerned, my wife had kindly arranged for sufficient funds or else we would have had to go back to India. And as far determination was concerned, I was ready to "sustain in the flight of life with the power of knowledge."

The Holy Qur'an says, "Proclaim! And thy Lord is Most Bountiful, He who taught (the use of) the pen, taught man which he knew not." And elsewhere it says, "Oh Lord, increase me in my knowledge."

CHAPTER 4
OPENING UP ABOUT ABUSE

*"Say, O My servants who have transgressed against themselves
[by sinning], do not despair of the mercy of Allah."*
—The Holy Qur'an 39:53

I think I was about 10 or 11 years old. It was the time of annual com-
memoration of the holy Prophet's birth. During the nights, *hadith*
would be read and *qaseeda* (poetry in praise of the holy Prophet,
peace be on him) reciters used to come and recite in our relatives'
homes in Madras (now known as Chennai) – in fact they would use
the *chabootara* (raised platform) in front of the houses, the place
would be lit by a petromax gas light as there was no electricity in
many of the houses. From our house and the adjacent mosque, we
would have to walk through an unlit and unpaved street – there were
trees on the way: mango, tamarind, wood apple – a *patrah* (iron smith
shop) owned by relatives and a pond too (about two times the size of
a basketball court). Not far away from those houses, there was a *neem*
tree too with its own *chabootra* of Cuddapah stone slab – this area too
was not so well lit. We would gather there with our acquaintances and
friends. Once when no one was so close by, a distant male relative
of mine about 10 years older than me, pulled me closer and force-
fully groped my left breast for at least a couple of minutes – I was a
young boy who had never been exposed to such indecent behaviour.
It was certainly a disgusting and a sickening incident that remains in

memory though I don't keep recollecting this incident or other such incidents – of course such incidents have shaped me to become a tough person who would gladly jump into unchartered waters to resist injustice or wrongs. By the way, the molestation left a swelling on my chest and remained there for years.

It was sometime in the academic year of 1961–62 when I was in my fifth form of high school (second year out of three years of high school). I was young and handsome. At school, I was a cadet in NCC's (National Cadet Corps) Naval wing. We went for an 8-10 day camp in Trichrapally (in Madras State, now in Tamil Nadu State). One night when we were about to go to bed, a classmate (and a cadet too) asked me to go with him. I did not know what he wanted but I followed him to a secluded place in the camp area. Let me point out at this time that we were brought up in such a manner and etiquette that demanded that we did not know how to say 'no' or question 'why' when someone demanded something from us – it would simply be disrespectful. Anyway, at the secluded place, the boy who was much older than me, embraced me and would not let me go – he offered me some colourful bougainvillea leaves as a 'gift'. After a few minutes, I finally got away from him. The next year, I never went for such a camp held in Srirangam (Madras State).

During the academic years ranging from 1964 through 1969, when I was in engineering school in Annamalai University (Madras state), I was a resident in a university hostel. We had four male students in a room, then as we advanced into fourth and final year of engineering there would be three in a room. During the second year of my studies there, I awakened one night to realize that my roommate was lying on my mattress and hugging me. I told him I wasn't interested and he left. Later on, in a group of few friends, in which that roommate was also present, I conveyed somewhat harshly that someone wanted to abuse me.

Again, during the second year of studies, another classmate who was residing a few rooms away from mine, and who used to exhibit his interest in me, came over to my sleeping spot. We used to put our mattresses on the *verandah* just outside the rooms. I told him I wasn't interested. He did not do anything but stayed there for a quite a long time. During the third year too, he remained interested but I used to avoid talking to him. He used to live like a dejected man. Such desires perhaps emanated from the unavailability of sexual outlets for young men of 17 to 21 years of age. I don't think there were any brothels in the town and interaction with the other sex was almost impossible as female students studying in other courses had their own hostels on the university campus and were not accessible to male students. At that time, in our engineering courses, there were no female students. So for the young students there were no 'dates' or girlfriends at least in that university campus.

Final year was a tougher one. Once when I woke up in the middle of the night, I realized that my roommate was in my cot closely hugging me. These cots made for 'single occupancy' were made out of bamboo frame with coir rope knitted around the frame. The guy was kissing me with his tongue in my mouth - there was a stinking smell. I sent him back to his cot. As I have indicated, in our final year, we would have three persons in a room and the other roommate was decent in a sense that he never approached me, so when this other roommate was present the 'stinking smell roommate' would never dare to venture towards my cot. But on the weekends, the decent roommate would return late in the night and on occasions when he was away, I wouldn't have proper sleep out of fear that the stinking roommate would approach me.

What motivates me to speak openly? I think it is part of my nature to tell the truth (because of my upbringing and other happenings that moulded me). When someone asks – I can't lie – and basically, I am open about my life stories and during conversations with friends and family, I sort of 'brag' about past interesting stories. I avoid thinking or talking about the abuse that I suffered as they are obviously not pleasant memories. One of the editors of this book (Shamsia) asked me to write as to what motivated me to raise my voice against the sanctions. I started thinking, of course seriously, as to why do I jump into causes to resist wrongs and it dawned on me that the very thing that I am trying to forget – namely abuse – is at the root of my psychological makeup and personality and therefore, I do raise my voice as and when needed. I have previously indicated that the hardships and struggles after migrating to Canada have further pushed me to act against injustices and the sanctions.

CHAPTER 5
CORRESPONDENCE WITH THE GOVERNMENT

*"My Lord, put my heart at peace for me and make my task
easy for me and remove the knot from my tongue, that they may
understand my speech."*
—The Holy Qur'an 20:25,26,27,28

State of mind when corresponding with government officials
That was a period of struggle in Halifax after migrating from Saudi
Arabia after the first Gulf War – in early 1994. Our business was not
very successful and the money we brought from Saudi Arabia was
draining fast. I was desperately trying to secure a job. After many years,
I finally secured a job in the City of Halifax related to my engineering
profession, however, which fetched me the bare minimum wage of $8
per hour – even that was a great relief to me financially and otherwise
too. So, naturally, I was in a state of mind that could be described as
consisting of frustration, anger, dislike of the system that brought
capable immigrants into Canada and left them just like that. Anything
wrong around me would enhance those feelings and strengthened my
natural inclination to fight wrongs as much as I can.

The Quranic verse that means to say that we are the best nation
brought out for people to command good and stop wrong has always
played a role in my life, and also the *hadith*, which means to say that

evil flourishes if good people don't stop wrong and destroys the good people too. Also, that was a time wherein I was close to a knowledgeable and well-known religious scholar, Dr. Jamal Badawi and was able to strengthen my belief in Islam and its teachings. I used to keenly participate in his *tafseer* sessions and invariably used to raise a question after every session and those answers were valuable. It certainly strengthened my soul and my actions too, and I would never give up any thing that I began. That was the time when the sanctions in Iraq were taking a real toll. I came across an organization Nova Scotia Campaign to End Iraq Sanctions (NSCEIS), and it appealed to me immensely as they were resisting the wrong.

My accumulated feelings of frustration, anger, dislike for wrong and of course my strengthened soul gave me the motivation, strength, and courage of conviction to raise my humble voice against sanctions in my own capacity in the form of letters to the editor and letters to the Ministers, etc.

This chapter outlines my correspondence in my attempts to persuade the Canadian government. It highlights the work I did, in my humble capacity, to work on opposing the sanctions regime by utilizing the media and working with NSCEIS. All letters and emails have been included as appendices.

Correspondence

7 February, 1998: The core issues contained in my letter dated 7 February, 1998 addressed to Prime Minister Jean Chrétien are about the impact of sanctions on Iraq, resulting in the death of children at an alarming rate, and about the US initiative to strike again militarily against Iraq. The Prime Minister's response dated 26 March, 1998 prepared by Keith Hanash, Special Assistant – Correspondence does not seem to address these issues at all.

20 March, 2000: Receive an email from L.A. Lavell, Executive Correspondence Officer to the Prime Minister. We can see that the

destructive issue of innumerable deaths due to the Iraq sanctions has been easily dispensed off by shoving the matter to the Minister of Foreign Affairs.

20 March, 2000: I bring the issue of sanctions to the attention of Bill Graham, chairman of the SCFAIT *(Standing Committee on Foreign Affairs and International Trade)*. Their response dated 21 March, 2000 indicated that my letter will be translated and circulated to the members of the committee for their consideration.

1 April, 2000: I remind Lloyd Axworthy, Minister of Foreign Affairs, about my letter dated 19 March, 2000 addressed to the Prime Minister and cc'd to him, and also said to have been forwarded to Axworthy by the Prime Minister's office.

Mohammed Javed
852 Old Sackville Road
Lower Sackville, N.S.
B4E 1R1
Phone: (902) 865-9354
Fax: (902) 864-5011
e-mail: mjaved3647@aol.com
7 February 1998

Honourable Jean Chretien
Prime Minister of Canada
Office of the Prime Minister
Ottawa, Ontario
K1A 0A2

Honourable Prime Minister:

I am writing this letter to bring to the kind attention of the just and honourable Prime Minister of Canada, the unjust US initiative to strike militarily against Iraq. I am sure Canada would not like to endorse or back this initiative to further destroy a nation that has already been destroyed systematically, forced into starvation, misery and cruel death under the disguise of embargo and sanctions.

Here are some miserable realities staring at us and demanding justice:

1. Mortality directly attributed to sanctions imposed on Iraq stands more than 1.2 million.
2. Iraq's under 5 children die at the rate of 6,500 every month.
3. Those over five die at the rate of 18,000.

Would we be able to bear the burden of a 1.2 million mortality?
Would we be able to bear the burden of younger children dying at the rate of 6,500 every month?
Would we be able to bear the burden of older children dying at the rate of 18,000?

No, we will not be able to bear the burden of seeing one single child dying of malnutrition in those pathetic conditions.

Then, why should the children of Iraq die?
Why should Iraq bear the burden of pathetic mortality?
Can we stay out of this slaughter of humanity?
Can we not protest?
Can we not grief?

Sincerely,

m. Javed

Mohammed Javed

Office of the
Prime Minister

Cabinet du
Premier ministre

Ottawa, Canada K1A 0A2

March 26, 1998

Mr. Mohammed Javed
852 Old Sackville Road
Lower Sackville, Nova Scotia
B4E 1R1

Dear Mr. Javed:

On behalf of the Right Honourable Jean Chrétien, thank you for your letter regarding the situation in Iraq.

The government is encouraged by the agreement reached between the Iraqi government and the United Nations, and we appreciate the diplomatic efforts of the Secretary General, Kofi Annan. Any deal, however, will need to be tested. As Canada has always preferred a diplomatic resolution to this matter, we remain hopeful that Saddam Hussein will comply with his obligations under UN resolutions.

Thank you for taking the time to write.

Sincerely,

Keith Hanash
Special Assistant - Correspondence

```
Subj: Sanctions Iraq - Web
Date: Mon, 20 Mar 2000 10:20:19 AM Eastern Standard Time
From: "Prime Minister" <pm@pm.gc.ca>
To:   mjaved3647@aol.com
CC:   mina10@dfait-maeci.gc.ca
```

Dear Mohammed Javed:

On behalf of the Right Honourable Jean Chrétien, I would like to thank you
for your e-mail, in which you raised an issue which falls within the
portfolio of the Honourable Lloyd Axworthy, Minister of Foreign Affairs. The
Prime Minister always appreciates receiving mail on subjects of importance to
Canadians.

Please be assured that the statements you made have been carefully reviewed.
I have taken the liberty of forwarding your e-mail to Minister Axworthy so
that he too may be made aware of your comments. I am certain that the
Minister will give your views every consideration.

L.A. Lavell
Executive Correspondence Officer
Agent de correspondance
de la haute direction

```
>>> <mjaved3647@aol.com> 19-03-00 11:09:54 AM >>>
reason          :Register criticism of government initiative
MESSAGE         :The Rt. Honourable Jean Chretien:
```

My Government, the Government of 30 million peace loving Canadians, the
Government of Liberals, the Government of Honourable Lloyd Axworthy and the
Government of Rt. Honourable Jean Chretian, in the process of parroting U.S
Government, supports the deadly U.N sanctions that kill 200 innocent,
starving, deprived, gloomy and pathetic Iraqi children every single day and
have left more than a million such children dead.

Will I or any of the millions of Canadians that include the Honourable
Axworthy and Rt. Honourable Jean Chretian dare to bear the burden of seeing
their pet animal, leave alone their own child, being cruelly starved to
death? No Sir, we will not bear that burden unless we are deaf, dumb and
blind and our hearts have been sealed and the souls are dead.

Will my Government, the Government of 30 million peace loving Canadians, the
Government of Liberals, the Government of Honourable Axworthy and the
Government of Rt. Honourable Chretian dare to tell the truth to the U.S
Government loudly and clearly that Canada Cannot bear the burden of death and
destruction of innocent Iraqi Children.

Rt. Hounarable Pime Minister, I do apologize for my harsh language but the
words have come out of my heart and I don't want to hide them. I am sure this
will be the loud and clear voice of 30 million Canadians if only they know
the truth! I wish they do know the truth!

```
Thanking you and with best regards Sir,

Sincerely,

Mohammed Javed, P.Eng.
852, Old Sackville Road
Lower Sackville, Nova Scotia
B4E 1R1, Canada
Phone: (902) 865-9354, Fax: (902) 864-5011
e-mail: mjaved3647@aol.com

firstname                  :Mohammed
lastname                   :Javed
address1                   :852, Old Sackville Road
address2                   :Lr. Sackville
city                       :Lr. Sackville
province                   :N.S
postcode                   :B4E 1R1
telephone                  :(902) 865-9354
fax                        :(902) 864-5011
email                      :mjaved3647@aol.com
guestbook                  :YES
Additional Information :
IP Address                 :152.168.61.201
DNS                        :98a83dc9.ipt.aol.com
Browser                    :IE 3.0
URL                        :/mail room/contact pm/index.asp
Created at                 :3/19/00 11:03:03 AM
```

Dear Mr.
    Thank-you for your comments regarding the sanctions against Iraq.
Please be assured that your letter will be translated and circulated to
members of the committee for their consideration.

Janice Hilchie
Clerk of the Standing Committee on Foreign Affairs and International
Trade
Greffière du Comité des affaires étrangères et du commerce international
tel. 613-996-1540; fax 613-996-1962

-----Original Message-----
From: Graham, Bill - M.P.
Sent: March 20, 2000 6:10 PM
To: Hilchie, Janice
Subject: FW: End Iraq Sanctions

-----Original Message-----
From: MJaved3647@aol.com [mailto:MJaved3647@aol.com]
Sent: Monday, March 20, 2000 5:02 PM
To: GrahaB@parl.gc.ca
Subject: End Iraq Sanctions

The Chairman of the SCFAIT,
Bill Graham,
Room 261 Confederation Building,
Ottawa, Ont.
Fax: 613-996-9607

Dear Sir,

Here is a presentation for SCFAIT:

My Government, the Government of 30 million peace loving Canadians, the
Government of Liberals, the Government of Honourable Lloyd Axworthy and the
Government of Rt. Honourable Jean Chretian, in the process of parroting U.S
Government, supports the deadly U.N sanctions that kill 200 innocent,
starving, deprived, gloomy and pathetic Iraqi children every single day and
have left more than a million such children dead.

Will I or any of the millions of Canadians that include the Honourable
Axworthy and Rt. Honourable Jean Chretian dare to bear the burden of seeing
their pet animal, leave alone their own child, being cruelly starved to

The Chairman of the SCFAIT,
Bill Graham,
Room 281 Confederation Building,
Ottawa, Ont.
Fax: 613-996-9607

Dear Sir,

Here is a presentation for SCFAIT:

My Government, the Government of 30 million peace loving Canadians, the Government of Liberals, the Government of Honourable Lloyd Axworthy and the Government of Rt. Honourable Jean Chretian, in the process of parroting U.S Government, supports the deadly U.N sanctions that kill 200 innocent, starving, deprived, gloomy and pathetic Iraqi children every single day and have left more than a million such children dead.

Will I or any of the millions of Canadians that include the Honourable Axworthy and Rt. Honourable Jean Chretian dare to bear the burden of seeing their pet animal, leave alone their own child, being cruelly starved to death? No Sir, we will not bear that burden unless we are deaf, dumb and blind and our hearts have been sealed and the souls are dead.

Will my Government, the Government of 30 million peace loving Canadians, the Government of Liberals, the Government of Honourable Axworthy and the Government of Rt. Honourable Chretian dare to tell the truth to the U.S Government loudly and clearly that Canada Cannot bear the burden of death and destruction of innocent Iraqi Children.

Rt. Hounarable Pime Minister, I do apologize for my harsh language but the words have come out of my heart and I don't want to hide them. I am sure this will be the loud and clear voice of 30 million Canadians if only they know the truth! I wish they do know the truth!

Thanking you and with best regards Sir,

Sincerely,

Mohammed Javed, P.Eng.
852, Old Sackville Road
Lower Sackville, Nova Scotia
B4E 1R1, Canada
Phone: (902) 865-9354, Fax: (902) 864-5011
e-mail: mjaved3647@aol.com

Subj: **Iraq sanctions**
Date: 4/1/2000 12:36:39 PM Atlantic Standard Time
From: MJaved3647
To: axworthy.l@parl.gc.ca
CC: pm@pm.gc.ca

Honourable Lloyd Axworthy:

This is with reference to my e-mail dated 19 March, 00 concerning U.N sanctions against Iraq, Canada's support for it parroting U.S Government that kills about 200 innocent Iraqi children every single day. The e-mail was addressed to Rt. Honourable Jean Chretien with a copy to you and was also forwarded to you from the PM's office as the issue falls within your jurisdiction. May I respectfully remind that I have not yet received your response.

Thanking you and with best regards,

Sincerely,

Mohammed Javed, P.Eng.
852, Old Sackville Road
Lr. Sackville, N.S.
B4E 1R1
Phone: (902) 865-9354
Fax: (902) 864-5011
e-mail: mjaved3647@aol.com

1 April, 2000: I send a reminder to Bill Graham, MP and Chairman of SCFAIT. I receive a response from Marie Danielle Vachon on 9 April, 2000 stating that in response to my enquiry the committee met on 6 April, 2000 to consider a draft resolution concerning their examination of sanctions against Iraq. The resolution was adopted in the committee and will become public once it has been tabled in the House of Commons. In the meantime, they direct my attention to committee meetings 29, 30, and 32 particularly.

10 April, 2000: I respond to the SCFAIT letter by saying that I have seen the documents pertaining to the said meetings, and I do not see any tangible developments to end the sanctions.

12 April, 2000: Receive an email from Svend Robinson, a prominent MP representing NDP. He said he is writing with positive news concerning the hearings of the SCFAIT on the situation in Iraq. The committee held public hearings. On 12 April, 2000 the committee tabled their report in the House of Commons. The email contained an extract from a speech by Svend Robinson in the House of Commons.

He made it clear in his speech that it is not acceptable that the Iraqi people should be victimized in this way (through the sanctions). He calls for the support for the resolution, the bill tabled before the House on 12 April 2000. The key recommendation of SCFAIT was a call for: "... urgently pursuing the 'delinking' of economic from military sanctions with a view to rapidly lifting economic sanctions, in order to significantly improve the humanitarian situation of the Iraqi people ..."

The email contained an oral question posed by Svend Robinson in the House of Commons (3 April, 2000) and response by the Honourable Lloyd Axworthy. It also contained the FIFTH REPORT of SCFAIT submitted to House of Commons by Bill Graham.

Subj: **FW: Iraq sanctions**
Date: 4/9/2000 5:18:45 PM Atlantic Daylight Time
From: VachoM@parl.gc.ca (Vachon, Marie Danielle)
To: MJaved3647@aol.com ('MJaved3647@aol.com')

Dear Mr. Javed,

Your e-mail of April 1 to Mr. Bill Graham, Chair of the Standing Committee on Foreign Affairs and International Trade has been forwarded to me for response.

In response to your enquiry, the Committee met April 6 to consider a draft resolution concerning their examination of sanctions against Iraq.

The resolution was adopted in Committee and will become public once it has been tabled in the House of Commons; a copy will be forwarded to you at that time.

In the interim, you may wish to consult the Committee website at www.parl.gc.ca, I direct your attention to meetings number 29, 30 and 32 particularly.

On behalf of the Chair, Mr. Graham, and of Committee members, I wish to thank your for your interest in the work of the Committee.

Marie Danielle Vachon,
Clerk

Subj: **Iraq Sanctions**
Date: Mon, 10 Apr 2000 10:58:46 AM Eastern Daylight Time
From: MJaved3647
To: vachom@parl.gc.ca

Dear Marie:

This is further to my e-mail dated 9 April, 00 that was in response to yours of the same date. As suggested by you I have seen the documents pertaining to meetings 29, 30 and 32. I don't see any tangible development to end sanctions or end parroting U.S Government on this issue. It looks that it will just turn out to be another futile exercise falling on the deaf ears of our Government. May I know as to the fate of presentation that I sent to the Chairman of the Committee, Mr. Bill Graham. And may I respectfully remind him through this e-mail that I need to have an answer from him. Thanks.

With best regards,

Sincerely,

Mohammed Javed

Subj: Iraq
Date: 4/12/2000 5:45:56 PM Atlantic Daylight Time
From: Robinson.S@parl.gc.ca (Robinson, Svend - M.P.)
To: mjaved3647@aol.com ('mjaved3647@aol.com')

House of Commons
OTTAWA
PLEASE QUOTE FILE: S00-9910

April 12, 2000

Dear Friends:

I am writing with positive news concerning the hearings of the Standing
Committee on Foreign Affairs on the situation in Iraq. At my urging,
following my visit to Iraq with a delegation from the Montreal-based group
Voices of Conscience/Objection de Conscience in January, the Committee
agreed to hold public hearings on this important issue. We heard from a
broad range of eloquent witnesses from across Canada and beyond, including
former UN Humanitarian Coordinator in Iraq Denis Halliday. I want to thank
all of those who appeared before the Committee for their excellent evidence.
On April 12, the Committee tabled our report in the House of Commons. I am
very pleased to enclose a copy of the Committee report, which you will note
was adopted unanimously by the Committee.

As with any report that is the subject of debate and compromise, there was
give and take. It is certainly not the report that I would have written
myself...for example, I would have included references to the impact of the
illegal and devastating bombing in the north and south, and the effects of
depleted uranium, as well as a much clearer call to support those who are
working for human rights and democracy in Iraq. I outlined a number of
these concerns in a recent speech in the House, and I enclose an extract for
your information.

"We can also look at another context, a context of what many of us believe
is effectively genocidal policies. That is the context of what is taking
place in Iraq today. It is what has been taking place over the past decade
under the imposition of United Nations sanctions which have resulted in the
death of over 500,000 innocent children. This has been well documented by
UNICEF and other international tribunals. It has been eloquently denounced
by the former UN humanitarian co-ordinator, Denis Halliday, eloquently and
passionately denounced by his successor, Hans von Sponeck, who has announced
his resignation.
I had the privilege of meeting with Hans von Sponeck when I visited Iraq
along with a delegation from a group called Objection de Conscience or
Voices of Conscience. They pointed out the combined impact of the
destruction of Iraqi infrastructure from bombing in the spring of 1991, the
ongoing bombing which is taking place illegally by the U.S. and the United
Kingdom, and the massive starvation of innocent civilians, children and
others, malnutrition used as a weapon of war against innocent children.
Dr. Sheila Zurbrig of Halifax, one of the world's experts on this subject,
has made it very clear that this is a breach of the most fundamental
international obligations which exist. The Geneva conventions say that we
cannot use malnutrition and starvation as a weapon of war, yet that is what

is happening in Iraq.

I want to be very clear. This is certainly not suggesting that we should not be calling on Saddam Hussein to account for his crimes against humanity. We all know of the terrible attacks on the Kurds, the gassing of Kurds in Halabja and elsewhere, but it is not acceptable that innocent Iraqi people should be victimized in this way, allegedly in order to attack Saddam Hussein.

Denis Halliday said that we are destroying an entire society. It is as terrifying and as simple as that.

We call for support for this resolution, this bill before the House today. At the same time I would appeal to our government to recognize that we should not be a part of the genocidal policies in Iraq ourselves. We should be using our position of leadership as we preside this month at the security council to call for a de-linking of military and economic sanctions, for the immediate lifting of economic sanctions, for an end to the illegal bombing in the north and the south, for the opening of a Canadian embassy in Iraq and for regional disarmament in that deeply troubled region."

But as you will observe, the key recommendation of the Committee is a call for:

"...urgently pursuing the "de-linking" of economic from military sanctions with a view to rapidly lifting economic sanctions, in order to significantly improve the humanitarian situation of the Iraqi people..."

This is coupled with a call to re-open our Canadian Embassy in Baghdad, and to pursue the issue of regional disarmament, consistent with paragraph 14 of UN Resolution 687.

This Resolution will now be forwarded to the Minister of Foreign Affairs, Lloyd Axworthy. Canada is presiding this month at the Security Council. On April 3, I called in the House on the Minister to finally show leadership on this issue at this critical time. I enclose a copy of that exchange for your information.

I urge you to contact the Minister and request him to act on the unanimous report of the Standing Committee now. Also, contact your own MP and ask them to speak out on this issue. We can make a difference.

Honourable Lloyd Axworthy, PC, MP
Minister of Foreign Affairs
418-N Centre Block
House of Commons
Ottawa, Ontario K1A 0A6
Axworthy.L@parl.gc.ca

First Name Last Name
House of Commons
Ottawa, Ontario
K1A 0A6
Lastname.Firstinital@parl.gc.ca (e.g. Robinson.S@parl.gc.ca)

Sincerely yours,

Svend J. Robinson, M.P.

SJR/sbm
PASS
Enclosures

ORAL QUESTION
House of Commons
April 3rd, 2000

Mr. Svend J. Robinson (Burnaby-Douglas, NDP): Mr. Speaker, my question is for the Minister of Foreign Affairs.
Canada will preside this month at the security council with a focus on human security. Will Canada finally speak up for the security of the people of Iraq, where over 500,000 children have died since 1990 as a result of inhumane UN sanctions? Will Canada call for the immediate lifting of these genocidal sanctions as recommended by former UN humanitarian co-ordinators Denis Halliday and Hans von Sponeck? Will we stop calling for studies and call for action to lift these sanctions now?

Hon. Lloyd Axworthy (Minister of Foreign Affairs, Lib.): Mr. Speaker, as the hon. member probably knows, there was an agreement reached this weekend to provide additional access to $250 million for new equipment to go into Iraq so it can expand its oil pumping capacity.
Furthermore, one of the initiatives we have taken is to do a major review of all sanctions policy, including a case study of Iraq. We will be tabling this at the security council in about mid-April and then asking the council to have a major examination debate on the application and utility of sanctions, both the effect on the humanitarian civil side and how it tries to compel the behaviour to the standards of the United Nations. It is that balance that we have to maintain as part of the Canadian approach to human security.

HOUSE OF COMMONS
CANADA

The Standing Committee on Foreign Affairs and International Trade has the honour to present its	Le comité permanent des affaires étrangères et du commerce international a l'honneur de présenter son
FIFTH REPORT	**CINQUIÈME RAPPORT**

In accordance with its mandate under Standing Order 108(2), your Committee has considered the issue of sanctions against Iraq and has agreed to report the following:

Conformément au mandat que lui confère le paragraphe 108 (2) du Règlement, votre Comité a examiné la question des sanctions contre l'Iraq et a convenu de rapporter ce qui suit :

Stressing the need to address on an urgent basis the ongoing humanitarian tragedy in Iraq;

Soulignant la nécessité de remédier à titre urgent à la tragédie humanitaire en cours en Irak;

Recalling the actions of the Iraqi regime of Saddam Hussein in the 1980s and early 1990s, including the use of weapons of mass destruction against both Kurdish Iraqi citizens and Iran, the pursuit of a clandestine nuclear weapons capability despite being a signatory to the Non-Proliferation Treaty, the invasion of neighbouring Kuwait and missile attacks on Israel;

Rappelant que, pendant les années 1980 et au début des années 1990, le régime irakien de Saddam Hussein a, entre autres, utilisé des armes de destruction massive contre les citoyens irakiens kurdes et l'Iran, cherché à se doter d'une capacité nucléaire clandestine alors que l'Irak est signataire du Traité de non-prolifération, envahi le Koweït voisin et lancé des attaques au missile contre Israël;

Recalling the decisions of the United Nations Security Council to take all necessary measures to reverse the invasion of Kuwait and ensure the complete disarmament of Iraq's weapons of mass destruction and their delivery systems, involving the imposition of a broad sanctions regime;

Rappelant que le Conseil de sécurité des Nations Unies a décidé de prendre toutes les mesures nécessaires pour annuler l'invasion du Koweït et assurer la neutralisation complète des armes de destruction massive de l'Irak et de leurs systèmes de lancement, par l'imposition d'un régime de sanctions d'application générale;

Noting the establishment of a UN Oil-For-Food program to allow the sale of Iraqi oil, yet aware that the cumulative effects of the broad sanctions regime continues to impose tremendous hardship upon the people of Iraq while not effectively weakening the government of Saddam Hussein;

Prenant acte de l'établissement par l'ONU d'un programme pétrole-contre-nourriture permettant la vente de pétrole irakien, mais conscient que les effets cumulatifs du régime de sanctions d'application générale imposent toujours d'énormes privations au peuple de l'Irak sans affaiblir pour autant le gouvernement de Saddam Hussein;

Welcoming the January 1999 Security Council adoption of a Canadian suggestion to establish expert panels to look at the issues of disarmament, the humanitarian situation and Kuwaiti prisoner of war and reparations issues as a means of breaking a growing impasse in the Security Council;

Accueillant avec satisfaction l'adoption par le Conseil de sécurité en janvier 1999 d'une suggestion canadienne de charger un groupe d'experts d'examiner les questions du désarmement, de la situation humanitaire, des prisonniers de guerre koweïtiens et de la restitution des biens koweïtiens comme moyen de dénouer l'impasse croissant au Conseil de sécurité;

Noting the March 1999 report of the UN expert panel on humanitarian issues entitled Report of the second panel established pursuant to the Note by the President of the Security Council on 30 January 1999 (S/1999/100) concerning the current humanitarian situation in Iraq, which noted in paragraphs 43 and 49, inter alia, that

Notant que, dans son rapport de mars 1999 intitulé Rapport du deuxième groupe d'experts établi comme suite à la note du président du Conseil de sécurité en date du 30 janvier 1999 (S/1999/100) concernant la situation humanitaire actuelle en Irak, le groupe d'experts de l'ONU sur les questions humanitaires déclare aux paragraphes 43 et 49, entre autres, que

the country has experienced a shift from relative affluence to massive poverty…infant mortality rates in Iraq today are among the highest in the world…chronic malnutrition affects every fourth child … only 41% of the population have regular access to clean water…the gravity of the humanitarian situation of the Iraqi people is indisputable and cannot be overstated;

le pays est passé d'une relative aisance à la pauvreté massive (…) le taux de mortalité infantile de l'Irak compte parmi les plus élevés au monde (…) la malnutrition chronique affecte un enfant sur quatre (…) seulement 41 % des habitants jouissent d'un accès régulier à une eau propre (…) la gravité de la situation humanitaire du peuple irakien est indiscutable et ne saurait être exagérée;

Deeply concerned by evidence presented to the Committee that in the past year the humanitarian situation in Iraq has in fact seriously deteriorated;

Noting the March 1999 report of the UN expert panel on disarmament entitled Report of the first panel established pursuant to the Note by the President of the Security Council on 30 January 1999 (S/1999/100) concerning disarmament and current and future ongoing monitoring and verification issues, which noted in paragraphs 25 and 27, inter alia, both that "The bulk of Iraq's proscribed weapons programmes has been eliminated," and that "... 100% of verification may be an unattainable goal;"

Taking note of Security Council Resolution 1284, adopted in December 1999, and the significant role Canada played in the adoption of this resolution, which has the potential, according to UN Secretary- General Kofi Annan, to "enhance the impact of the program in alleviating the humanitarian situation in Iraq," but which, according to certain witnesses, will not, even if implemented, enable Iraq to create the economic conditions necessary for ending the humanitarian crisis;

Welcoming the appointment as the Executive Chairman of the new UN Monitoring, Verification and Inspections Commission (UNMOVIC) of Dr. Hans Blix, and underlining the requirement for cooperation by the Iraqi regime in carrying out the work of the Commission;

Having met with experts, including former UN Assistant Secretary- General and UN Humanitarian Coordinator in Baghdad, Denis Halliday, and Canadian NGOs concerned with and knowledgeable about the current situation in Iraq;

Profondément inquiet des témoignages qu'il a reçus à l'effet que la situation humanitaire en Irak s'est en fait détériorée au cours de la dernière année;

Notant que, dans son rapport de mars 1999 intitulé Rapport du premier groupe d'experts établi comme suite à la note du président du Conseil de sécurité en date du 30 janvier 1999 (S/1999/100) touchant les activités actuelles et futures de contrôle et de vérification, le groupe d'experts de l'ONU sur le désarmement déclare aux paragraphes 25 et 27, entre autres, à la fois que « le gros des programmes d'armes proscrites de l'Irak ont été éliminés » et que « la vérification à 100 % est peut- être un objectif inatteignable »;

Prenant acte de la résolution 1284 du Conseil de sécurité adoptée en décembre 1999 et du rôle important que le Canada a joué dans l'adoption de cette résolution, qui est susceptible, d'après le Secrétaire général de l'ONU Kofi Annan, « de rehausser la capacité du programme à améliorer la situation humanitaire en Irak », mais qui, selon certains témoins, même si elle est appliquée, ne permettra pas à l'Irak de créer les conditions économiques nécessaires pour mettre fin à la crise humanitaire;

Accueillant avec satisfaction la nomination du Dr Hans Blix au poste de président- directeur de la nouvelle Commission de contrôle, de vérification et d'inspection des Nations Unies (COCOVINU) et soulignant la nécessité pour le régime irakien de coopérer à l'exécution du travail de la Commission;

Ayant rencontré les experts, dont l'ancien Secrétaire général adjoint de l'ONU et coordonnateur des affaires humanitaires à Bagdad Dennis Halliday, et des ONG canadiennes informées et préoccupées de la situation actuelle en Irak;

Convinced of the urgency of the humanitarian situation in Iraq, and noting testimony that a "de-linking" of economic from military sanctions against Iraq would significantly improve the humanitarian situation in Iraq while satisfying security concerns;

Aware that the Government of Canada is pursuing the study of reforming the system of sanctions during its April 2000 presidency of the UN Security Council;

The Standing Committee on Foreign Affairs and International Trade recommends that the Government of Canada:

Reaffirm publicly the need to address on an urgent basis the ongoing humanitarian tragedy in Iraq;

Notwithstanding the adoption of Security Council Resolution 1284, urgently pursue the "de-linking" of economic from military sanctions with a view to rapidly lifting economic sanctions in order to significantly improve the humanitarian situation of the Iraqi people, while maintaining those aspects of the multilateral embargo necessary to satisfy security requirements and contribute to the overall goal of regional disarmament;

Establish a Canadian diplomatic presence in Iraq in order to monitor developments in that country more effectively and to make direct representations to the Government of Iraq;

Continue to pursue the broader issue of the reform of the use of sanctions in order to allow a clearer targeting of military forces and regimes instead of civilian populations.

Convaincu de l'urgence de la situation humanitaire en Irak et notant les témoignages suivant lesquels le fait de dissocier les sanctions économiques des sanctions militaires prises contre l'Irak améliorerait grandement la situation humanitaire en Irak tout en répondant aux impératifs de sécurité;

Conscient que le gouvernement du Canada poursuit l'étude de la réforme du système des sanctions pendant sa présidence en avril 2000 du Conseil de sécurité de l'ONU;

Le Comité permanent des affaires étrangères et du commerce international recommande que le gouvernement du Canada :

Réaffirme publiquement la nécessité de remédier à titre urgent à la tragédie humanitaire en cours en Irak;

Nonobstant l'adoption de la résolution 1284 du Conseil de sécurité, cherche de façon urgente à faire dissocier les sanctions économiques des sanctions militaires en vue de lever rapidement les sanctions économiques dans le but d'améliorer sensiblement la situation humanitaire du peuple irakien tout en maintenant les aspects de l'embargo multilatéral nécessaires pour satisfaire aux impératifs de sécurité et contribuer à l'objectif global de désarmement régional;

Établisse une présence diplomatique canadienne en Irak de manière à mieux suivre l'évolution de la situation dans ce pays et à intervenir directement auprès du gouvernement de l'Irak;

Poursuivre l'étude plus large de la réforme du recours aux sanctions de manière à pouvoir mieux cibler les régimes et les forces militaires plutôt que les populations civiles.

A copy of the relevant Minutes of Proceedings (Meetings Nos 30, 32 and 34) is tabled.

Un examplaire des procès- verbaux pertinents (réunions n°s 30, 32 et 34) est déposé.

Respectfully submitted,

Respectueusement soumis,

Le président,

Bill Graham
Chair

12 April, 2000: I send a reminder to Lloyd Axworthy, Minister of Foreign Affairs, requesting him to take action on the unanimous report of SCFAIT that was tabled in the House of Commons on 12 April 2000.

26 April, 2000: I send a thank you email to Peter Stoffer, an NDP MP for his telephone call concerning the Iraq sanctions.

26 April, 2000: L.A. Lavell, Executive Correspondence Officer to Prime Minister Jean Chrétien acknowledged the receipt of my email, dated 21 April, 2000 and 'assured' me in his email that my comments have been carefully noted. My said email was addressed to the editor of *The Chronicle Herald, The Mail Star* and cc'd to the Prime Minister – the pet dog of a nine-year-old girl was shot which devastated her, and I wrote in the letter that the sanctions have devastated not one or two but a million parents as a million children have perished. The letter was published on 4th May, 2000 under title 'Cruelly Punished'.

18 May, 2000: I forward a copy of my letter that I wrote to the editor of *Chronicle Herald* to Art Eggleton, Minister of Defence. The letter, titled 'What a contrast', was published in the newspaper on 22 May, 2000. It was about *HMCS Calgary* getting ready to set sail to the Arabian Gulf to enforce the sanctions.

Subj: **Iraq sanctions**
Date: 4/12/2000 8:20:23 PM Atlantic Daylight Time
From: MJaved3647
To: axworthy.l@parl.gc.ca
CC: pm@pm.gc.ca, grahab@parl.gc.ca
CC: robinson.s@parl.gc.ca, stoffp@parl.gc.ca
CC: newsroom@herald.ns.ca

Honourable Lloyd Axworthy:

1. This is with reference to my e-mail dated 19 March, 00 concerning Canada's support for U.N sanctions against Iraq that kill 200 innocent Iraqi children every single day. The e-mail was addressed to Rt. Honourable Jean Chretien with a copy to you and was also forwarded to you from the PM's office as the issue falls within your jurisdiction. May I respectfully remind you, sir, that I have not yet received your response.

2. I am also respectfully urging you to act forthwith on the unanimous report of the Standing Committee on Foreign Affairs (comprising Mr. Bill Graham, M.P., Mr. Svend Robinson, M.P., etc.) that was tabled today (12 April, 00) in the House of Commons. Sir, as you know the report recommends that the Government of Canada reaffirm publicly the need to address, on an urgent basis, the on going human tragedy in Iraq.

3. Every single day of inaction adds 200 dead children to the obituary list of the million innocent ones who pathetically perished in their death beds for no fault of theirs but unfortunately could not move the soul less U.S Government nor the parroting Canadian Government. The heart and souls of 30 million peace loving Canadians, for sure, are not dead!

Thanking you and with best regards sir,

Sincerely,

Mohammed Javed, P.Eng.
852, Old Sackville Road
Lr. Sackville, N.S.
B4E 1R1
Phone: (902) 865-9354
Fax: (902) 864-5011
e-mail: mjaved3647@aol.com

Subj: **Thanks**
Date: 4/26/2000 7:34:48 AM Atlantic Daylight Time
From: MJaved3647
To: stoffp@parl.gc.ca

Mr. Peter Stoffer
Member of Parliament

Dear Peter Stoffer:

Thanks for your telephone message and concern for the children and civilians of Iraq even though you are not my Member of Parliament. In fact it should be a matter of concern for all Canadians as their Government has been instrumental in systematically destroying not only innocent children but an entire society. I would appreciate if you would kindly forward my earlier letter to my Member of Parliament.

Thanking you sir and with best regards,

Sincerely.

Mohammed Javed

Subj: **Iraq Sanctions**
Date: 4/26/2000 3:46:54 PM Atlantic Daylight Time
From: pm@pm.gc.ca (Prime Minister)
To: MJaved3647@aol.com

Dear Mohammed Javed:

On behalf of the Right Honourable Jean Chrétien, I wish to acknowledge receipt of your recent e-mail.

I would like to thank you for writing to the Prime Minister and assure you that your comments have been carefully noted.

L.A. Lavell
Executive Correspondence Officer
Agent de correspondance
de la haute direction

>>> <MJaved3647@aol.com> 21-04-00 9:11:40 AM >>>
Dear Editor:

It is early Friday morning in Halifax on April 21 in the new millineum. The Chronicle Herald portrays a large picture 'our sins'. It also reports in bold headlines the shooting death of Patricia's pet dog. For sure, it devastates the tender, emotional nine year old girl because her innocent pet is not only dead but has been cruelly shot dead.

Somewhere else, not very far away, on our own planet, in a place called Iraq, a million innocent children, pets of their parents have died and continue to die because of the cruel UN sanctions dictated by U.S. Government and vigourously supported by our Canadian Government. It devastates not one or two but a million parents because their innocent pet children have been cruelly punished to death. Does it devastate the Honourable Lloyd Axworthy and Rt. Honourable Jean Chretien too? I do not know the answer to this question but what I do know is that recently Mr. Axworthy has announced 'generously' a million dollar humanatarian aid to Iraq. Is it 'blood money' at the rate of $1 per dead pet child or is it an atonement of the sin? Will Mr. Axworthy answer this single million dollar question honestly? Sir, if Canada had answered it rightly, if U.S. had answered it rightly, a million children would not have perished pathetically and the dog too! A million parents and Patricia would not have been devastated! How sad!

Sincerely,

Mohammed Javed, P.Eng.
852, Old Sackville Road
Lr. Sackville, N.S.
B4E 1R1
Phone: (902)865-9354
Fax: (902)864-5011
e-mail: mjaved3647@aol.com

Subj: **Ship of Shame**
Date: 5/18/00 7:30:59 AM Atlantic Daylight Time
From: MJaved3647
To: egglea@parl.gc.ca

Honourable Art Eggleton
Minister of Defence

Here is a letter that I wrote to the editor Chronicle Herald and should be of concern to you, sir.

Thanking you and with best regards,

Mohammed Javed

The Editor
Chronicle Herald

Dear Editor:

This year, during the summer of new millennium, Canada from its East Coast will witness an impressive event when the Tall Ships 2000 that have already set sail on a challenging adventurous & constructive run will arrive at the port of Halifax.

This year, during the same summer of new millennium, Canada from its West Coast will witness an obscure event when the mighty war ship of Canadian Navy HMCS Calgary, flexing its muscles, will set sail on a non-challenging, non-adventurous & destructive run towards the Arabian Gulf. The mission is to continue to enforce the deadly, 10-year old, Canadian supported UN sanctions against Iraq. Yes, the same sanctions that kill 200 innocent Iraqi children every day.

The Tall Ships 2000 will celebrate the run of the millennium. What will Art Eggleton's Calgary celebrate? The murder of a million innocent Iraqi children? What a comparison! What a contrast! Are we the humanity of the new millennium?

Mohammed Javed
852, Old Sackville Road
Lower Sackville, Nova Scotia
B4E 1R1, Canada
Phone: (902) 865-9354
Fax: (902) 864-5011
e-mail: mjaved3647@aol.com

3 June, 2000: I send 13 unsightly pictures of dying Iraqi children to the Prime Minister, cc'ing the *Chronicle Herald* and Svend Robinson.

12 June, 2000: I receive a response from Lloyd Axworthy, Minister of Foreign Affairs. Axworthy wrote about security concerns, which were unsubstantiated and were only perceived. He said, "To date, Iraq has refused to allow UN inspectors into the country in accordance with UN Security Council Resolution 1284 adopted on December 17, 1999. Canada believes that the situation requires sustained vigilance by the international community and the continuation of sanctions until Iraq is in full compliance with its Security Council Obligations."

Axworthy talked about two initiatives to address the humanitarian situation since Canada joined the UN Security Council in January 1999. During the April 2000 presidency of the Council, Canada announced the creation of a Security Council working group on sanctions policy with a mandate to develop recommendations on how to improve the effectiveness of UN sanctions, including a mandate to avoid negative humanitarian impacts. Also, Canada announced a one million dollar contribution UNICEF and the International Committee of the Red Cross to assist Iraq in rehabilitation.

Axworthy concludes by saying, "In pursuit of an end to the Iraq crisis, Canada will continue its efforts to establish a constructive dialogue with the Iraqi government in hopes of encouraging its compliance with its UN Security Council obligations." He wants to pursue this path and at least acknowledges that the situation has gone on for too long for the Iraqi people. We don't see anything substantial but some softening of stand, albeit insufficient, is visible from the Minister's response – at least in words.

Subj: **Horrors of Iraq sanctions - in pictures**
Date: 6/3/00 2:48:13 PM Atlantic Daylight Time
From: M.Javed3647
To: pm@pm.gc.ca, axworthy.l@parl.gc.ca
CC: newsroom@herald.ns.ca
CC: end-sanctions@chebucto.ns.ca, grahab@parl.gc.ca
CC: robinson.s@parl.gc.ca, cic@cicnow.com

File: PIC1.ZIP (376012 bytes)
DL Time (44000 bps): < 2 minutes

Rt. Honourable Jean Chretien,
Honourable Lloyd Axworthy:

Would you please see the attached 13 un-sightly pictures of dying innocent Iraqi children. The havoc, the horror, the misery, the tyranny, the genocide, the destruction and the death on a million such children is unleashed by the U.N sanctions dictated by U.S and supported by your Canada. Please stop it for heaven sake (hope you believe in one). Sir, would you? Thanks.

Sincerely,

Mohammed Javed
852, Old Sackville Road
Lr. Sackville, N.S.
B4E 1R1
Phone: (902) 865-9354
Fax: (902) 864-5011
e-mail: mjaved3647@aol.com

Subj: A-07417-00 In reply to your E-mail of April 12, 2000
Date: 6/12/00 3:32:04 PM Atlantic Daylight Time
From: min.dfaitmaeci@dfait-maeci.gc.ca
To: mjaved3647@aol.com

June 9, 2000

Mr. Mohammed Javed, P.Eng.
mjaved3647@aol.com

Dear Mr. Javed:

Thank you for your e-mail of April 12, 2000, concerning the humanitarian situation in Iraq. Unfortunately, my office had no record of receiving your previous message on this issue.

Canada believes that there remain serious security concerns surrounding Iraq's pursuit of nuclear, chemical and biological weapons. The United Nations Security Council (UNSC) imposed sanctions against Iraq in order to deal with these concerns. To date, Iraq has refused to allow UN inspectors into the country in accordance with UN Security Council Resolution 1284 adopted on December 17, 1999. Canada believes that the situation requires sustained vigilance by the international community and the continuation of sanctions until Iraq is in full compliance with its Security Council obligations.

However, the Canadian government shares your concern regarding the humanitarian situation faced by the Iraqi people and we have taken measures aimed at alleviating the hardships being faced by them. During our April 2000 presidency of the UN Security Council, Canada announced the creation of a Security Council working group on sanctions policy with a mandate to develop recommendations on how to improve the effectiveness of UN sanctions. The working group has a mandate to explore ways of targeting sanctions and avoiding negative humanitarian impacts. Also in April, Canada announced a $1 million contribution to UNICEF and the International Committee of the Red Cross to assist them in the rehabilitation of primary schools, hospitals and primary health care centres in the south and centre of Iraq, as well as the repair and maintenance of water treatment plants. While Iraq's announced refusal of this assistance was frustrating, Canadian assistance will be distributed by international non-governmental organizations and not the Government of Iraq.

These two initiatives are consistent with continuing Canadian efforts to address the humanitarian situation since we joined the United Nations Security Council in January 1999. At that time, weapons inspections had stopped and there was no consensus on what path the Council should take next. Canada broke the impasse by proposing the establishment of three panels to study the humanitarian, disarmament and Kuwaiti prisoner situations in Iraq. Their recommendations subsequently became the basis for the December 17, 1999, Security Council Resolution 1284 on Iraq.

Resolution 1284 addresses many of Canada's concerns. The establishment of the new weapons inspection agency, UNMOVIC, addresses our disarmament and security concerns. On the humanitarian front, Resolution 1284 provides for a number of key humanitarian provisions which can be implemented without requiring reciprocal Iraqi concessions. These provisions include the lifting of the ceiling on oil exports, the addition of a cash component to humanitarian contracts to help with local implementation, and a streamlined approval process for humanitarian goods. The oil export ceiling has been lifted and Iraq now controls the quantity of its oil exports. The pre-approved list of goods in the food, education, medical and agricultural sectors has been implemented by the Security Council. Full compliance by the Iraqi regime with its Council-mandated obligations would trigger an automatic lifting of sanctions, alleviating the suffering of the Iraqi people.

On April 12, 2000, the Standing Committee on Foreign Affairs and International Trade released a resolution on Iraq. This resolution acknowledged the steps Canada has taken to date to improve the humanitarian situation in Iraq and urged the Government to pursue the de-linking of economic from military sanctions with a view to rapidly lifting economic sanctions. The fast-track provisions of Resolution 1284 provides an effective lift of controls on a range of civilian items and Canada and other Security Council members remain committed to the further extension of these lists of exempted items, but we will remain vigilant regarding the export to Iraq of dual use items.

In pursuit of an end to the Iraq crisis, Canada will continue its efforts to establish a constructive dialogue with the Iraqi government in hopes of encouraging its compliance with its UN Security Council obligations. By pursuing this path, Canada hopes to bring an end to a situation which has gone on for too long. Too long for regional and international security. Too long for the Iraqi people.

Thank you again for writing.

Sincerely,

Lloyd Axworthy

22 June, 2000: I receive an email from Svend Robinson consisting of the House of Commons debate of 13 June, 2000. Svend asked the government of Canada to respond positively to the unanimous report by SCFAIT calling for the immediate lifting of economic sanctions against Iraq.

27 June, 2000: I forward to Svend Robinson the 12 June, 2000 email response from Lloyd Axworthy.

28 June, 2000: Svend Robinson responds to me that there is much work ahead of us to put an end to economic sanctions.

18 August, 2000: I enquire with Svend Robinson if Lloyd Axworthy has responded to the SCFAIT report tabled in the House of Commons on 12 April 2000.

21 August, 2000: Svend Robinson responds in an email that the Minster of Foreign Affairs had not yet responded to the SCFAIT report.

Subj: Iraq
Date: Thu, 22 Jun 2000 11:53:06 AM Eastern Daylight Time
From: "Robinson, Svend - M.P." <Robinson.S@parl.gc.ca>
To: "'mjaved3647@aol.com'" <mjaved3647@aol.com>

HOUSE OF COMMONS - DEBATES
CANADA
June 13th 2000

IRAQ - War Crimes

Mr. Svend J. Robinson (Burnaby-Douglas, NDP): I want to touch on two other areas. First, as I noted in the debate at second reading in the context of the discussion on war crimes, crimes against humanity and genocide, the global community must recognize that the impact of years of sanctions on the people of Iraq has been nothing short of genocidal.

UNICEF has documented the death of over half a million children. The infrastructure in that country has been destroyed. The bombing continues today. Innocent civilians are being killed. The impact of depleted uranium particularly in the south remains devastating. In the context of this debate I want once again to appeal to the Government of Canada.

I want to ask our government to respond positively to the unanimous report by the Standing Committee on Foreign Affairs and International Trade calling for the immediate lifting of economic sanctions against Iraq.

The foreign affairs committee held hearings on this issue. We heard compelling and moving evidence about the impact of the sanctions on the people of Iraq. I visited that country in January of this year along with a delegation from a group called Voices of Conscience. I met with former UN humanitarian co-ordinator, Hans Van Sponeck. I met with Denis Halliday, his predecessor.

All of them are pleading with the community of nations, with the United Nations, with our government, with Canada, to recognize the appalling and inhumane impact of these sanctions on innocent human people. Saddam Hussein is not being touched by these sanctions but innocent lives are being lost. The standing committee on foreign affairs issued a strong and unanimous report calling for the de-linking of economic and military sanctions. Yet to date we have had no response whatsoever from the foreign minister or from the Government of Canada.

I appeal today to the Government of Canada to respond before the House rises positively to that report, to listen to the voices of Canadians from coast to coast who are demanding that our government stand up and be counted in the security council and call for an end to these genocidal and inhumane sanctions. I appeal to our government to respond to that strong, positive and unanimous report of the foreign affairs committee at the earliest possible time.

Subj: Re: Iraq
Date: Tue, 27 Jun 2000 02:24:59 PM Eastern Daylight Time
From: MJaved3647
To: robinson.s@parl.gc.ca

Mohammed Javed
852, Old Sackville Road,
Lr. Sackville, N.S.
B4E 1R1
Phone: (902) 865-9354
Fax: (902) 864-5011
e-mail: mjaved3647@aol.com

Mr. Svend Robinson, M.P.

Dear Sir,

In response to my letter concerning Iraq sanctions and asking Lloyd Axworthy
to act on the SCFAIT resolution of April 12, 00, he has replied with an
e-mail. This would be of interest to you and I am reproducing it which is as
follows:

Subj: A-07417-00 In Reply to your E-mail of April 12, 2000
Date: 6/12/00 3:32:04 PM Atlantic Daylight Time
From: min.dfaitmaeci@dfait-maeci.gc.ca
To: mjaved3647@aol.com

June 9, 2000

Mr. Mohammed Javed, P.Eng.
mjaved 3647@aol.com

Dear Mr. Javed:

Thank you for your e-mail of April 12, 2000, concerning the humanitarian
situation in Iraq. Unfortunately, my office had no record of receiving your
previous message on this issue.

Canada believes that there remain serious security concerns surrounding
Iraq's pursuit of nuclear , chemical and biological weapons. The United
Nations Security Council (UNSC) imposed sanctions against Iraq in order to
deal with these concerns. To date Iraq has refused to allow UN inspectors
into the country in accordance with UN Security Council Resolution 1284
adopted on December 17, 1999. Canada believes that the situation requires
sustained vigilance by international community and the continuation of
sanctions until Iraq is in full compliance with its Security Council
obligations.

However, the Canadian government share your concern regarding the
humanitarian situation faced by the Iraqi people and we have taken measures
aimed at alleviating the hardships faced by them. During our April 2000
presidency of UN Security Council, Canada announced the creation of a
Security Council working group on sanctions policy with a mandate to develop
recommendations on how to improve the effectiveness of UN sanctions. The

working group has mandate to explore ways of targeting sanctions and avoiding negative humanitarian impacts. Also in April, Canada announced a $1 million contribution to UNICEF and the International Committee of the Red Cross to assist them in the rehabilitation of primary schools, hospitalsand primary health care centres in the south and centre of Iraq, as well as the repair and maintenance of water treatment plants. While Iraq's announced refusal of this assistance was frustrating, Canadian assistance will be distributed by international non-governmental organizations and not the Government of Iraq.

These two initiatives are consistent with continuing Canadian efforts to address the humanitarian situation since we joined the United Nations Security Council in January 1999. At that time weapons inspections had stopped and there was no consensus on what path the Council should take next. Canada broke the impasse by proposing the establishment of three panels to study the humanitarian, disarmament and Kuwaiti prisoner situations in Iraq. Their recommendations subsequently became the basis for the December 17, 1999, Security Council Resolution 1284 on Iraq.

Resolution 1284 addresses many of Canada's concerns. The establishment of the new weapons inspection agency, UNMOVIC, addresses our disarmament and security concerns. On the humanitarian front, Resolution 1284 provides for a number of key humanitarian provisions which can be implemented without requiring reciprocal Iraqi concessions. These provisions include the lifting of the ceiling on oil exports, the addition of a cash component to humanitarian contracts to help with local implementation, and a streamlined approval process for humanitarian goods. The oil export ceiling has been lifted and Iraq now controls the quantity of its oil exports. The pre-approved list of goods in the food, education, medical and agricultural sectors has been implemented by the Security Council. Full compliance by the Iraqi regime with its Council-mandated obligations would trigger an automatic lifting of sanctions, alleviating the suffering of the Iraqi people.

On April 12, 2000, the Standing Committee on Foreign Affairs and International Trade released a resolution on Iraq. This resolution acknowledged the steps Canada has taken to date to improve the humanitarian situation in Iraq and urged the Government to pursue the de-linking of economic from military sanctions with a view to rapidly lifting economic sanctions. The fast- track provisions of resolution 1284 provides an effective lift of controls on a range of civilian items and Canada and other Security Council members remain committed to the further extension of these lists of exempted items, but we will remain vigilant regarding the export to Iraq of dual use items.

In pursuit of an end to Iraq crisis, Canada will continue its efforts to establish a constructive dialogue with the Iraqi Government in hopes of encouraging its compliance with its UN Security Council obligations. By pursuing this path, Canada hopes to bring an end to a situation which has gone on for too long. Too long for regional and international security. Too long for the Iraqi people.

Thanking you again for writing.

Sincerely,

Lloyd Axworthy

Thanking you and with best regards,

Sincerely,

Mohammed Javed

Subj: **Iraq**
Date: 6/28/00 12:42:07 PM Atlantic Daylight Time
From: Robinson.S@parl.gc.ca (Robinson, Svend - M.P.)
To: MJaved3647@aol.com ('MJaved3647@aol.com')

OTTAWA   PLEASE QUOTE FILE: S00-28743

Mr. Javed,

Thank you for sending me this response from Lloyd Axworthy. Indeed, we still have much work ahead of us to put an end to economic sanctions.

Sincerely,

Svend Robinson, MP
Burnaby-Douglas

Subj: Your report of April, 00
Date: Fri, 18 Aug 2000 08:25:05 AM Eastern Daylight Time
From: MJaved3647
To: robinson.s@parl.gc.ca

Dear Svend:

This is concerning SCFAIT report of April 12, 00 concerning Iraq sanctions, that was tabled in House of Commons. Would you kindly let me know if Mr. Axworthy has reasonably responded? For sure, he would have come up with some ready made excuses for not acting.

Thanking you and with best regards,

Sincerely,

Mohammed Javed, P.Eng.
852, Old Sackville Road
Lr. Sackville, N.S.
B4E 1R1
Phone: (902)865-9354
Fax: (902)864-5011
e-mail: mjaved3647@aol.com

26 September, 2000: Art Eggleton, Minister of Defence, responds to my email of 18 May, 2000 concerning the preparations to send *HMCS Calgary* to the Persian Gulf and about the sanctions against Iraq.

He devotedly parrots to justify the US imposed UN sanctions and the need for Maritime interdiction by saying (for example), "The deployment of *HMCS Calgary* is part of Canada's contribution to a maritime interdiction operation established in cooperation with our allies to monitor and enforce United Nations Security Council Resolutions concerning the import and export of various commodities."

13 October, 2000: In this letter, Lloyd Axworthy, Minister of Foreign Affairs responds to Bill Graham's (MP, Chair, Standing Committee on Foreign Affairs and International Trade) letter of 14 June, 2000

Concerning SCFAIT's recommendation of 12 April, 2000 regarding Canadian Policy toward Iraq. We could see some softening in Canada's stand, though unsubstantial and too little too late.

Some of the important statements from the email:

"Canada's policy toward Iraq has consistently been governed both by the Government's concern for the humanitarian plight facing the people of Iraq and our ongoing concerns about security and disarmament."

"However, in the short term, and until the International community lifts the sanctions, it is essential for us to remain focused on the humanitarian plight of Iraqi people."

"Months of negotiation at the Security Council led to the adoption of Resolution 1284. Canada worked hard throughout the process to ensure that the new resolution brought about humanitarian improvements for the Iraqi people, and the implementation of more targeted sanctions."

"The Committee's recommendation regarding de-linking economic and military sanctions is one that is raised frequently in the context of Iraq. Indeed, the Canadian Government supports the concept of "smarter" sanctions, i.e., sanctions that effectively target regimes while minimizing harm to civilian populations."

"In the case of Iraq, a major step towards this objective is taking place now as resolution 1284 called for the preparation of lists of humanitarian items in the educational, medical and agricultural fields that henceforth would be pre-approved and fast-tracked through the system, effectively lifting any controls on their importation by Iraq."

Subj: **HMCS CALGARY**
Date: 9/26/00 4:46:57 PM Atlantic Daylight Time
From: Eggleton.A@parl.gc.ca (Eggleton, Art - M.P.)
To: Mjaved3647@aol.com ('Mjaved3647@aol.com')

Dear Mr. Javed:

Thank you for your e-mail of May 18, 2000, concerning preparations to send Her Majesty's Canadian Ship (HMCS) CALGARY to the Persian Gulf and sanctions against Iraq. I apologize for the delay in responding.

The deployment of HMCS CALGARY is part of Canada's contribution to a maritime interdiction operation established in co-operation with our allies to monitor and enforce United Nations Security Council Resolutions concerning the import and export of various commodities. This includes the movement of weapons components and oil to and from Iraq. Canada has periodically sent ships to participate in maritime interdiction operations since 1991.

The sanctions regime was originally established by United Nations Security Council Resolution 687 in 1991. More recently, the Security Council established the United Nations Monitoring, Verification and Inspection Commission to undertake the responsibilities of the former United Nations Special Commission, which monitored the elimination of weapons of mass destruction-including biological and chemical weapons-in Iraq. As you may know, the Iraqi government has consistently refused to co-operate with the United Nations on this issue. The resolve of the Iraqi leadership to develop weapons of mass destruction is a matter of record, as is their willingness to use these weapons-even against their own people. Canada therefore joins with the international community to ensure that the sanctions regime and the Monitoring, Verification and Inspection Commission can effectively promote the security of the citizens of Iraq and of the region. Like you, the Government of Canada is deeply concerned about the adverse impact of sanctions on the Iraqi people. The Government is therefore working on initiatives to ensure that future sanctions are targeted at the country's leaders.

As a member of the United Nations Security Council for 1999-2000, Canada also supports the Council's intention to lift the sanctions once certain conditions have been met. United Nations Security Council Resolution 1284, adopted by the Security Council on December 17, 1999, states that, once the United Nations Monitoring, Verification and Inspection Commission and the International Atomic Energy Agency report that Iraq has been co-operating in all respects with their reinforced monitoring system for a period of 120 days, the sanctions will be suspended for 120 days. This suspension would be renewable by the Council and subject to Iraq's continued respect for United Nations prohibitions on its weapons production. Resolution 1284 also removes the ceiling for the export of Iraqi oil under the humanitarian program known as "Oil for Food," which expands the amount of humanitarian aid the Iraqi government may purchase. It is the Iraqi government alone that bears the responsibility for ensuring the well-being of its people, both through the distribution of humanitarian aid and through speedy compliance with Resolution 1284.

Maritime interdiction operations exist to enforce United Nations Security Council Resolutions, which are binding under international law. Canada's involvement in enforcement actions is designed to contain the proliferation of weapons of mass destruction and is consistent with its tradition of intervention in the name of peace.

Once again, thank you for your e-mail. I appreciate hearing your concerns on this matter.

Sincerely,

Art Eggleton

Minister of Foreign Affairs   Ministre des Affaires étrangères

Ottawa, Canada K1A 0G2

'OCT 1 3 2000

Mr. Bill Graham, M.P.
Chair
Standing Committee on Foreign Affairs
and International Trade
Room 637, 180 Wellington Street
Ottawa, Ontario
K1A 0A6

Dear Colleague:

Thank you for your letter of June 14, 2000, requesting a response by the Government to the recommendations presented by the Standing Committee on Foreign Affairs and International Trade on April 12, 2000, regarding Canadian policy toward Iraq. I would like to commend the Committee for its efforts on this very complex issue and thank you for the opportunity provided my officials to meet with the Committee and outline the rationale underlying Canada's approach to Iraq. The recommendations you have presented reflect the deep concerns we all share regarding the humanitarian situation in Iraq and our collective desire to improve the conditions being endured by the Iraqi people.

Canada's policy toward Iraq has consistently been governed both by the Government's concern for the humanitarian plight facing the people of Iraq and our ongoing concerns about security and disarmament. Canada's long-term objective is to work toward the suspension and eventual lifting of sanctions within a context that ensures Iraq's compliance with the UN Security Council's disarmament requirements, requirements imposed by the international community to safeguard the security of the region after the Iraqi invasion of Kuwait. The cooperation of the Iraqi regime with the United Nations and the resultant lifting of sanctions would create the best possible outcome not just for the Iraqi people, but for people in other nations in the region, some of which still harbour very serious security concerns about Iraq.

However, in the short term, and until the international community lifts the sanctions, it is essential for us to remain focussed on the humanitarian plight of the Iraqi people. Canada has provided approximately $37 million since 1991 in humanitarian assistance for the people of Iraq, through organizations such as the ICRC, UNHCR, World Food Programme, Canadian Foodgrains Bank, and UNICEF.

Canada has worked hard at the Security Council since our arrival in January 1999 to advance our concerns about the humanitarian situation in Iraq. As the Committee notes, at the suggestion of Canada, the Security Council established three panels to study the humanitarian concerns, disarmament and the Kuwaiti prisoner of war issues.

Months of negotiation at the Security Council led to the adoption of Resolution 1284. Canada worked hard throughout that process to ensure that the new resolution brought about humanitarian improvements for the Iraqi people, and the implementation of more targeted sanctions.

It is important to note that, while perhaps not perfect, Resolution 1284 represents the best possible consensus that could have been achieved at the Security Council. And, without the new resolution, all nations, including Canada, would still be bound under international law by the earlier resolutions.

The Committee's recommendation regarding de-linking economic and military sanctions is one that is raised frequently in the context of Iraq. Indeed, the Canadian government supports the concept of "smarter" sanctions, i.e., sanctions which effectively target regimes while minimizing harm to civilian populations. Much research and debate is taking place on how smarter sanctions can be developed and implemented.

In the case of Iraq, a major step towards this objective is taking place now as Resolution 1284 called for the preparation of lists of humanitarian items in the educational, pharmaceutical, medical and agricultural fields that henceforth would be pre-approved and fast-tracked through the system, effectively lifting any controls on their importation by Iraq. These lists will soon be augmented by the inclusion of a range of items in the water and sanitation sectors that will also receive pre-approval once the lists are finalised. Most importantly, however, the ceiling on oil exports was lifted. Under the previous ceiling, $3.4 billion was the maximum amount available for humanitarian spending but, due to low oil prices, this target was not met. With the ceiling lifted in Phase VII, approximately $4.8 billion was available for humanitarian spending, and the Office of Iraq Program is projecting expenditures of $7.1 billion in the current phase. This is more than double what was available before the ceiling was lifted. In his June 2000 report, Secretary-General Annan outlined positive developments in Phase VII (December 1999 to June 2000) of the humanitarian distribution program. These include the first distribution of targeted nutrition inputs for children and pregnant and lactating women; the provision of cold chain vehicles and equipment in the health sector; the containment of a threatened outbreak of polio; and the arrival of warehouse equipment and vehicles that will improve logistics in the health and education sectors. I remain hopeful - and moderately encouraged by the UN Secretary-General's June report - that the situation on the ground will improve as the improvements called for in Resolution 1284 work their way through the system to the people most affected.

Those items not included on these lists generally fall within a category of goods with clear dual-use capabilities (civilian and military applications), requiring continued monitoring by the UN Sanctions Committee. Canada believes continued vigilance on dual-use goods is prudent. Even in these areas, however, there has been increased flexibility demonstrated by some members of the Sanctions Committee in weighing the real risks associated with the importation by Iraq of certain items versus the positive impact they could have in improving the humanitarian conditions in Iraq. The decision to allow the importation of water purification materials is one recent example of this positive trend.

The sanctions system in Iraq extends beyond just controlling the flow of goods into Iraq. The cornerstone of the UN sanctions system in Iraq is the maintenance of financial controls on Iraq to ensure that revenues generated by oil exports–currently unlimited and generating revenues in excess of $16 billion/year– are spent on humanitarian goods and cannot be used to rebuild Iraq's weapons programs. It is not clear from the Committee's report whether these essential controls should also be removed as part of the "de-linking" process. If these controls are removed to allow for the free import by Iraq of all goods it deems necessary, the ability of the international community to control exports to Iraq would be severely degraded, relying in large measure on the goodwill of Iraqi purchasers or foreign suppliers to exert needed controls and Iraq's willingness to allow and cooperate with monitors. It would, in short, revert to the system that was in place in the period before the Gulf War when Iraq was able to build a threatening arsenal of proscribed weapons.

The Committee also recommended that Canada re-establish a Canadian diplomatic presence in Baghdad to more effectively monitor developments in Iraq.

Canadian diplomats based in Amman make regular visits to Iraq and we are in regular contact with Iraq-based diplomats and others in Amman who cover Baghdad. Moreover, we do maintain a high-level dialogue with senior Iraqi officials through our respective Permanent Representatives to the United Nations in New York. Of course, Canada's ultimate objective is to re-open the Canadian embassy in Baghdad, however, I believe that to do so now or to permanently station a Canadian diplomat in Iraq at this time would be premature. Nonetheless, Canada's relations with Baghdad are not static. In the last year, we have stepped up the frequency and seniority of Canadian officials who have gone into Iraq. Canada is hopeful that Iraq will re-integrate into the international community. We will continue to monitor our relations, and, when appropriate, we will take further measures to expand our communications and relations with the Iraq government.

I strongly welcome the Committee's recommendation that Canada continue to pursue the broader issue of sanctions reform with an eye towards the development of sanctions regimes that are better targeted. As you know, Canada has been leading the effort in the Security Council to make sanctions more effective and humane. For example, Canada sponsored a major independent study by the International Peace Academy on UN Sanctions with recommendations for improving the way sanctions are applied. As President of the Council in April, Canada chaired the first-ever open Council meeting on sanctions with a view to launching a process of review and reform of UN sanctions.

During this session Canada successfully pushed for the creation of a Council working group on sanctions policy to explore ways of mitigating the humanitarian impact of sanctions. The working group was requested to report back to the Council in November 2000 with across-the-board recommendations for improving the design, administration and implementation of sanctions. It is expected that the working group will develop guidelines and thus promote improvements in the way the Council devises sanctions regimes, particularly with regard to avoiding negative impacts on civilians.

Indeed, it is precisely these issues which the Committee might find interesting to pursue in a more in-depth and meaningful way. Given that the Committee does favour the imposition of sanctions in certain cases (e.g., SCFAIT resolutions on Burma, Fiji) and the diminution of sanctions in others (SCFAIT reports on Kosovo, Iraq), I would like to re-iterate and expand on a suggestion I made previously, which is that it might be useful and constructive if the Committee were to look at the instruments we have in Canada, such as SEMA, as well as multilateral instruments with a view to making some concrete proposals on how sanctions regimes can be reformed as to be better targeted. Under which circumstances should sanctions be imposed and how? I believe that the Committee could make a very positive and meaningful addition to the international debate and study that is currently underway in this area.

I hope that the foregoing addresses the key concerns expressed by the Committee on the question of Iraq. As I said at the outset, the Committee's hard work and diligence on the range of complex issues related to Iraq have added significantly to our on-going assessment both of the situation in Iraq and the broader sanctions issue. We will continue to closely monitor the situation in Iraq, focussing in particular on the humanitarian situation.

I would once again like to thank you and the Committee for your valuable views.

Sincerely,

Lloyd Axworthy

18 October, 2000: I send an email to NSCEIS (Nova Scotia Campaign to End Iraq Sanctions) about my meeting some ambassadors, MPs, senators, and journalists, and voicing concern about Iraq sanctions at a dinner and reception held at Parliament Hill in Ottawa on 16 October, 2000.

20 October, 2000: I receive an email addressed to me on behalf of the Chair, Bill Graham, and members of SCFAIT that they have tabled a resolution (FIFTH REPORT) in the House of Commons on 12 April, 2000. On 13 October, 2000, the Minister of Foreign Affairs provided a response to the Committee's report.

13 November, 2000: NSCEIS Steering Committee writes to Kofi Anan, Secretary General UN asking for his approval for their humanitarian flight proposal, "We intend to charter a plane destined for Baghdad in the first months of 2001 that will carry goodwill ambassadors carrying food, humanitarian and medical relief supplies."

14 November, 2000: I send an email to John McNee, Director General of the Middle East, North Africa and Gulf States Bureau Department of Foreign Affairs expressing concern about Iraq sanctions and about my article titled "An Undeclared Nuclear War" that was published in the *Chronicle Herald*.

15 November, 2000: John McNee responds, "The twin goals of Canada's policy remain humanitarian – a deep concern for the plight of the people of Iraq – and disarmament – the imperative to ensure through weapons inspection that Iraq will not again be in a position to threaten its neighbours and threaten security in the region."

Subj: **Ottawa Parliament Hill meeting**
Date: 10/18/00 7:48:19 PM Atlantic Daylight Time
From: MJaved3647
To: end-sanctions@chebucto.ns.ca

Hello NSCEIS all:

Had the opportunity of meeting some ambassadors, members of Parliament, senators and journalists and voiced concern about Iraq sanctions at a reception held at Parliament Hill in Ottawa on Monday night (Oct. 16, 00).

1. Svend Robinson was excited to learn about our proposed 'Canadians to Baghdad' relief flight and said, "Would you please see I have a place on this flight."

2. Met John McNee, former Canadian ambassador to Middle Eastern countries and present Director General in our Foreign Affairs Ministry. Iraq policy is under his jurisdiction and he seems to have much say in this. He appeared to be appreciateing the havoc the sanctions have caused. John McNee will be responding to our Chronicle Herald article 'An undeclared nuclear war.' He is also expected to discuss further with me on the sanctions issue.

3. Gordon Earle (M.P.) won't be in Halifax on Oct. 24 and therefore will not be able to attend the Pilger film event.

4. Talked to senator Marcel Prud'homme, P.C. and ambassadors from other countries concerning the sanctions. Thanks.

Mohammed

STANDING COMMITTEE ON FOREIGN
AFFAIRS AND INTERNATIONAL
TRADE

BILL GRAHAM, CHAIR, M.P. FOR ROSEDALE

HOUSE OF COMMONS
CHAMBRE DES COMMUNES
OTTAWA, CANADA
K1A 0A6

COMITÉ PERMANENT DES AFFAIRES
ÉTRANGÈRES ET DU COMMERCE
INTERNATIONAL

BILL GRAHAM, PRÉSIDENT, DÉPUTÉ DE ROSEDALE

October 20, 2000

Mr. Mohammed Javed
852, Old Sackville Road
Lower Sackville, NS
B4E 1R1

Dear Mr. Javed:

On behalf of the Chair, Bill Graham, and of Members of the Standing Committee on Foreign Affairs and International Trade, I wish to thank you for your interest in the Committee's recent study of sanctions against Iraq.

The Committee's hearings on this issue culminated with the tabling of a resolution in the House of Commons on April 12, 2000. On October 13, 2000 the Minister provided a response to the Committee's report, which I have enclosed for your information.

Again, on behalf of the Chair and of Members of the Standing Committee, I wish to thank you very much for your interest in the Committee's work.

Sincerely,

Marie Danielle Vachon
Clerk

Encl.

   Room / Pièce 637, 180 rue Wellington Street, Ottawa, Ont. K1A 0A6 Tel: 996-1540 / Fax: 947-9670

9 Raving Hill
Bedford, Nova Scotia
Canada. B4A 3L3
Phone: (902) 832-1641
Fax: (902) 864-5011
e-mail: : endsanctions@chebucto.ns.ca

November 13, 2000

Kofi Annan
Secretary General
United Nations

Dear Kofi Annan,

We are writing to you on behalf of Canadian human-rights activists, community leaders and politicians concerned about the impact of sanctions on Iraq.

These impacts, including the deaths of hundreds of thousands of Iraqis-most of them children-have been extensively documented in your organization's reports. They are a clear violation of the United Nation's Charter and international law.

We intend to charter a plane destined for Baghdad in the first months of 2001 that will carry goodwill ambassadors carrying food, humanitarian and medical relief supplies.

Having read UNSC resolution 670, we trust that this mission will meet with your approval. Should you have any questions or concerns, feel free to contact us.

Sincerely,

Nova Scotia Campaign to End the Iraq Sanctions Steering Committee members:

Dr. Betty Peterson

Sadik Khalal

Brooks Kind

Abdul Zora

Mohammed Javed

Daniel Haran

Qoutaiba H. Al-Qaysi

Subj: Response to your e-mail to John McNee Nov 15
Date: Mon, 20 Nov 2000 12:13:05 PM Eastern Standard Time
From: Dennis.Horak@dfait-maeci.gc.ca
To: MJaved3647@aol.com

Dear Mr. Javed,

The Director General of the Middle East and North Africa Bureau, Mr. John
McNee, has asked me to respond to your e-mail of November 15 conveying your
request for a more detailed response to your article "An undeclared Nuclear
War".

As you can well appreciate, there are many articles and op-ed pieces written
concerning Iraq in the Canadian media and academic circles. Most, like
yours, are thoughtful pieces providing useful insight and food for thought
in assessing developments in the region. We are grateful when the authors
draw our attention to articles they have written that might be of interest
to this Division. However, given the broad interest in the Iraq situation
in Canada, not to mention other regional issues for which we are
responsible, it would not be possible for us to respond directly to each and
every article written on the Iraq situation.

In his original response to your article, Mr. McNee noted that Canada's
policy on the Iraq situation is guided by the twin goals of seeking to
improve the humanitarian situation in Iraq and continued vigilance to ensure
that Iraq met its disarmament obligations. Canada believes firmly that the
balanced approach we would like to see applied to the Iraq situation is
reflected in UNSC Resolution 1284 passed last December by the UN Security
Council. We continue to believe that Iraq's cooperation with the UN offers
the best way forward for a resolution of both elements of the Iraq problem.

Once again, I would like to thank you for taking the time to forward your
interesting article to us.

Sincerely,

Dennis Horak
Deputy Director
Middle East Division

Subj: **Re: (no subject)**
Date: 11/15/00 5:44:57 PM Atlantic Standard Time
From: MJaved3647
To: john.mcnee@dfait-maeci.gc.ca

His Excellency John McNee:

Thank you very much for your response. I appreciate that you have shared my article (An Undeclared Nuclear War) with your colleagues in the Middle East Division. I would appreciate further if a response could be made either to me or to the Chronicle Herald by the concerned officials/Minister of Foreign Affairs concerning the issues that I have raised in the article. For sure, they are serious issues.

Thanking you and with best regards,

Sincerely,

Mohammed Javed, P.Eng.

In a message dated 11/15/00 10:03:32 AM Atlantic Standard Time, john.mcnee@dfait-maeci.gc.ca writes:

<< Dear Mr Javed.

Thank you for your message. I have shared your article with my colleagues in the Middle East Division who deal with Iraq. The twin goals of Canada's policy remain humanitarian--a deep concern for the plight of the people of Iraq--and disarmament--the imperative to ensure through weapons inspection that Iraq will not again be in a position to threaten its neighbours and threaten security in the region. Iraq's cooperation with the UN still offers the way to achieve both these important goals.

Yours sincerely, John McNee
>>

Subj: **RE: (no subject)**
Date: 11/15/00 10:03:32 AM Atlantic Standard Time
From: john.mcnee@dfait-maeci.gc.ca
To: MJaved3647@aol.com

Dear Mr Javed,

Thank you for your message. I have shared your article with my colleagues in
the Middle East Division who deal with Iraq. The twin goals of Canada's
policy remain humanitarian—a deep concern for the plight of the people of
Iraq—and disarmament—the imperative to ensure through weapons inspection
that Iraq will not again be in a position to threaten its neighbours and
threaten security in the region. Iraq's cooperation with the UN still offers
the way to achieve both these important goals.

Yours sincerely, John McNee

——Original Message——
From: MJaved3647@aol.com [mailto:MJaved3647@aol.com]
Sent: November 14, 2000 12:15 PM
To: john.mcnee@dfait-maeci.gc.ca
Subject: (no subject)

His Excellency John McNee
Director General
Middle East and North Africa
Department of Foreign Affairs and International Trade

His Excellency:

We have met at the annual reception and dinner of Canadian Islamic Congress
held on October 16, 00 in Ottawa. Hope you would have an opportunity to go
through my article "An Undeclared Nuclear War." We remain concerned about
the
continuing Iraq sanctions and the disaster it has created. Hope our
Government would initiate efforts to lift the sanctions.

Thanking you and with best regards,

Sincerely,

Mohammed Javed, P.Eng.
852, Old Sackville Road
Lr. Sackville, N.S.
B4E 1R1
Phone: (902) 865-9354
Fax: (902) 864-5011
e-mail: mjaved3647@aol.com

10 May, 2001: There was a debate in the House of Commons.

Mr. Svend Robinson (Burnaby-Douglas, NDP) brought forward a motion and moved:

"That in the opinion of this House the Canadian Government should lead efforts at the United Nations to lift the economic sanctions imposed upon Iraq since 1991, which have served only to inflict severe suffering on civilians, especially the most vulnerable members of the Iraqi population, namely the elderly, the sick and children."

Svend Robinson courageously, touchingly, and eloquently speaks the truth to describe the unimaginable sufferings, death, and destruction that Iraq has faced in the last ten years due to the genocide unleashed by UN sanctions, war, and relentless bombings.

Ms. Libby Davies (Vancouver East, NDP) supported the motion. She stated, "In closing, I want to thank the member for Burnaby-Douglas for bringing forward this issue again: a sane idea, a saner policy for a humane world where we do not destroy a civil society because we are trying to get at one person."

CANADA

HOUSE OF COMMONS DEBATES

DEBATE
May 10, 2001

Sanctions against Iraq

Mr. Svend Robinson (Burnaby—Douglas, NDP) moved:

> That, in the opinion of this House, the Canadian government should lead efforts at the United Nations to lift the economic sanctions imposed upon Iraq since 1991, which have served only to inflict severe suffering on civilians, especially the most vulnerable members of the Iraqi population, namely the elderly, the sick and children.

He said: Madam Speaker, it is with a sense of profound sadness and anger that I rise in my place in the House today to once again plead with our government, the Government of Canada, to finally show leadership and to call on the United Nations and on every other international forum for an end to the genocidal sanctions that have been imposed upon the people of Iraq for the last decade.

I cannot believe I am still standing in place today pleading with our government to act, over a year after a strong, powerful and eloquent report of a unanimous foreign affairs committee called on the Liberal government to do precisely what I am seeking today, to lift the economic sanctions that have had such a catastrophic impact on innocent human lives, innocent people in Iraq.

SVEND J ROBINSON, MP
BURNABY-DOUGLAS
366 WEST BLOCK, HOUSE OF COMMONS, OTTAWA, K1A 0A6
613-996-5597   ROBINS@PARL.GC.CA

The sanctions certainly have not had an impact on Saddam Hussein, but over the course of the last decade, they have resulted in the death, according to UNICEF, of over half a million children under the age of five.

I travelled to Iraq back in January 2000 with a delegation from a group called Voices of Conscience, Objection de conscience. This is a group of very fine women and men, mainly from Quebec, who are artists, journalists, doctors and representatives of non-governmental organizations. We travelled overland into Baghdad and then down into the southern part of Iraq.

For me it was a return visit because I had been to Iraq nine years previously, just before war broke out. I visited in November 1990 leading a delegation that included Lloyd Axworthy, then foreign affairs critic for the Liberal Party, and a Conservative member of parliament named Bob Corbett.

The results of the imposition of that draconian sanctioned regime, as well as the massive and ongoing bombings that many Canadians do not even know is happening in Iraq today, were absolutely devastating both to the people and to the infrastructure of Iraq.

We must never forget the appalling attack that took place in 1991. I will not call it a war because, as one of the United States generals said, it was like shooting fish in a barrel. I believe there were over 100,000 Iraqi casualties of that attack.

Prior to that attack, Iraq was one of the most advanced countries in the Middle East in economic, social and cultural rights. Iraq has the second largest oil reserves in the world after Saudi Arabia. They belong to the people of Iraq. They were nationalized in 1972. Iraq had an extensive health care system, clean and abundant drinking water, sewage treatment plants, electric power generation plants, free education at all levels and a comprehensive network of social services. The status of women in Iraq, a country in the Middle East in which too often women are still very much second class citizens, was one of the most advanced of any country in that region.

What our delegation witnessed on our return last year was the total collapse of Iraq's human and physical infrastructure, a nation that has experienced a shift from, as was described by the United Nations development program, relative affluence to massive poverty. Unemployment is epidemic. Inflation has skyrocketed. The average salary is about $5 U.S. a month. There has been a dramatic increase in begging, prostitution and crime.

The agriculture sector is in disarray, ravaged by hoof and mouth disease, screwworm and the effects of major drought. The once thriving and vibrant cultural sector has been another victim of this inhumane sanctions regime, as our delegation heard from the artists with whom we met.

While we were in Baghdad we also met with the then United Nations humanitarian co-ordinator, Hans von Sponeck. Hans von Sponeck, who was a distinguished public servant with the United Nations for many years, resigned shortly after we left. He said that he could no longer participate in the administration of the inhumane sanctions regime. In resigning in that way, he joined the former United Nations humanitarian co-ordinator, Dennis Halliday, and the former head of the United Nations World Food Program, Jutta Burghardt. He pointed out in many speeches afterwards that, in his words, Iraq was truly a third world country once again. He said, and I quote:

I have never been in a country where I have seen so many adults crying.

In a recent speech, he quoted from a December 2000 UNICEF report that ranked the increase in Iraq's child mortality rates the highest among 188 countries in the world since 1991, a 160% surge as a result of a lack of medicine, malnutrition and water borne diseases, such as dysentery.

Hans von Sponeck strongly opposes the sanctions and has called for the lifting of the sanctions. He said that he wants it clearly underlined that does not mean he supports Saddam Hussein, which is certainly also the case for myself and members of the New Democratic Party.

While Saddam Hussein has an appalling track record of repression, including the gassing of Kurds in northern Iraq at Halabja, and should be held accountable before the international community for his crimes, we also need to understand that the impact of these genocidal sanctions means that those are who are directly responsible for imposing them are, in my view, also guilty of crimes against humanity.

Let us look at the former United States secretary of state, Madeleine Albright. When she was asked in an interview whether the deaths of thousands and thousands of innocent Iraqi children were worth the price that was being paid to enforce these sanctions, she looked right into the camera and she said "yes, that is a price worth paying". That was a price worth paying, the death of those children.

As my colleague for Vancouver East said, that is shameful and that is genocidal. As Hans von Sponeck said "whether you die by bullets or by hunger and disease, you are still dead". Iraq in the last 10 years has suffered beyond any imaginable allowable limits.

We often hear talk of Iraq as a rogue state. The United States is seeking to justify its new star wars scheme, the national missile defence program, partly by suggesting that somehow Iraq, North Korea, Iran and others are rogue states.

I want to suggest that the true rogue state on the planet today in fact is the United States itself, which has shown such contempt for international law and for the standards of basic humanity in enforcing these profoundly immoral and illegal sanctions.

The United States, after all, is a country that has demonstrated contempt for international law in many different ways. It has shown contempt for the environment by turning its back on the Kyoto accord. It has shown contempt for the rights of children by being one of the only countries in the world, along with Somalia, that has refused to sign the international convention on the rights of the child. It has shown contempt for international law by supporting the absolute violent and appalling policies of the Israeli government in its attacks on the Palestinians and its illegal policy of occupation in settlements. Terrible violence is being directed against Palestinians. It is the United States that has consistently been propping it up. We can also look at the United States in the context of its support for the illegal sanctions against Cuba. Once again, which state is the real rogue state in the world today? We know which one it is.

The current situation in Iraq is absolutely tragic. The greatest burden of these sanctions is borne by the most vulnerable people in Iraqi society: the children, the women, the disabled and the elderly.

As I have mentioned, UNICEF has confirmed that infant mortality rates have skyrocketed since the imposition of these sanctions. Over half a million children have died as a result of the imposition of these sanctions and 4,500 children continue to die each month.

I met with doctors in Baghdad and Basra who, with tears in their eyes, spoke of their sense of helplessness and powerlessness in being unable to save the lives of more than 2% of the children in their care in the oncology wards. They knew that many of those who survived would just return to hellish conditions of malnutrition and open sewage. There was one nurse for 100 children in a ward that we visited.

There has been an explosive rise in the incidence of endemic infections, such as cholera, typhoid and malaria, and major increases in measles, polio and tetanus. Iraq has also seen a huge brain drain as a result of the sanctions. The middle class has largely been destroyed and young people see no hope for their future. We were told of Saturday auctions where proud Iraqi families are forced to sell off their family heirlooms and furniture simply to survive.

I visited a pediatric clinic in Basra in the south. The death toll there was particularly high and it was linked to the use by the allies of depleted uranium in bombing in the spring of 1991. As I have mentioned, the bombings continue even today in that region. It is illegal. The no fly zones have no legal basis whatsoever, yet the United States and the U.K. continue to bomb and innocent civilians continue to die as a result of that bombing. Recently they

bombed just outside Baghdad. I was ashamed as a Canadian that our government was one of the only governments that was actually prepared to stand up and defend the United States and the United Kingdom in that illegal bombing. The bombing goes on and the impact of depleted uranium in terms of the congenital deformities, particularly in the south, has been terrible.

We also witnessed the results of what one Baghdad professor referred to as the intellectual genocide of Iraq. Virtually no funding is left for education as a result of the oil proceeds and so the system has collapsed. They have no access to scientific and medical journals and no opportunities to attend professional conferences. Parents give their children chalk to take to schools. Our delegation brought their children pencils and medical supplies as an act of silent defiance.

What about the oil for food program? Well, it has not worked. In fact the so-called 661 committee, which enforces the program, has been harshly criticized by many commentators, including the secretary general of the United Nations who said just last November that he had serious concerns over the excessive number of holds that have been placed on applications and on sectors, such as electricity, water, sanitation and agriculture, that impact adversely on the poor state of nutrition in Iraq.

I would like to say a word about nutrition. Dr. Sheila Zurbrigg has documented eloquently the state of famine that has gripped Iraq today. She pointed out that in recent statistics the trends in mortality are getting even worse and that the conditions are getting worse. She also said that child malnutrition rates in the centre south part of the country do not appear to have improved and nutrition problems remain serious and widespread. Acute malnutrition is a huge problem and it is above 10%. Many children are small for their age and visibly wasting away. One in seven Iraqi children will die before the age of five. It is absolutely unbelievable. The agricultural sector, as the FAO has pointed out, is in crisis as well.

I have mentioned Dr. Sheila Zurbrigg. I will also pay tribute to the many Canadians, individuals and organizations that have worked so tirelessly and with such commitment and dedication against these inhumane and genocidal sanctions. These include the Canadian Network to End Sanctions on Iraq, the Nova Scotia Campaign to End Iraq Sanctions, End the Arms Race, Physicians for Global Survival Canada, Objection de conscience or Voices of Conscience, Project Ploughshares, Kawartha Ploughshares and many such groups across the country.

In closing, I once again remind the House of the unanimous recommendation of the Standing Committee on Foreign Affairs and International Trade that the government immediately work for the lifting of economic sanctions. It is essential that the sanctions be lifted, that they be lifted now and that Canada show the leadership that makes it possible.

Ms. Libby Davies (Vancouver East, NDP): Madam Speaker, I am pleased to rise in the House today to wholeheartedly support the motion brought forward by the member for Burnaby—Douglas.

The work of the member for Burnaby—Douglas has been outstanding, not just on this issue but also in understanding and promoting international human rights. He speaks with a great sense of hope for people in Canada who seek an alternative to Canada's foreign policy. The member has been a beam of light for a lot of people in in the work that he has undertaken.

I listened with great sadness as he described his personal visit to Iraq and what he encountered while there.

Members in the House and Canadian enjoy the basic necessities of life, although there are people in this country who live in poverty. However what is happening to the people of Iraq is something that is truly horrifying.

I listened to the debate and was quite alarmed at what I heard. The member who spoke for the government side and the member who spoke for the Canadian Alliance were both members of the committee and, as we heard from the member for Burnaby—Douglas, were part of the unanimous report that came from that committee which sought to have these sanctions removed.

It quite alarming that in a committee members can somehow find the courage and the reason to see the absolute horror and devastation of what has happened with the sanctions, yet on another day in the House somehow be in favour of them. In fact the member for the Alliance characterized the motion as being naive. I am quite surprised by that. If we look at the impact of these sanctions, which have been in place for over a decade, on a civilian population, we see nothing less than the total destruction of a civil society.

If we followed the Alliance member's reasoning and logic, if we can call it a logic, then for the net result what would be success in the eyes of that member? Would it be that every child has died? Would it be that 50% of the population of children under five have died? The logic of what is being presented is actually illogical.

I take issue with the fact that, as we have heard, the target of the sanctions is Saddam Hussein. If that is so, then there has to be an agreement that the goal of those sanctions has been a failure. Here we are 10 years later and the guy is still in power. Meanwhile the civil society, the infrastructure, the hospitals, the health care, the water system and everything has been totally destroyed. I would say to those who have been proponents of this kind of course of action and this kind of foreign policy that this has been an abject failure.

In my community of Vancouver east, and in Vancouver generally, I have received many letters and phone calls from individual constituents who have been

horrified and outraged at the destruction these sanctions have caused the people of Iraq.

I have personally attended rallies, vigils and meetings. I know that some of the real activists in Vancouver, people like Linda Morgan who was very involved in organizing the delegation that went to Iraq last year, are very committed to an international campaign of solidarity with people from other countries to draw attention to what is taking place in this country. As a Canadian member of parliament, I feel ashamed that our government has so blindly followed this sanction policy for so many years.

Let us be clear about what the motion before us today says. It does not say that Canada should take unilateral action. It does not say that Canada should just strike out on its own. It says that the Canadian government should lead the efforts at the United Nations to lift economic sanctions. There are many Canadians who would see that as a positive, hopeful and powerful role for the government to play rather than standing by and watching the devastation take place.

I listened to the news the other day to hear what was going on, as we all do every day. I made note that the Pope has now called for lifting of the sanctions. I believe there is a growing consciousness globally that if this is what we have sunk to as an international community, if the lowest common denominator of foreign policy is to basically impose hunger, famine, lack of medical supplies, lack of education, lack of clean water and if this is what foreign policy has come to, then where are we in terms of an international community?

As Canadians we should pause and reflect about our complicity is in these sanctions. I urge members on the government side, particularly those members who are part of the foreign affairs committee and who apparently supported the lifting of the sanctions, to think about what this government policy is doing.

It seems to me that historically after a conflict or war there is often a period of reconciliation where the international community comes together to rebuild from the devastation of war. Yet in this situation not only was there a war that was horrific, and we could argue that another day in terms of what that was all about, but another war has unfolded, a war that has been even more devastating and that has been going on now for 10 years, which is the war of these sanctions.

Therefore, I feel a sense of deep tragedy about what has taken place here. I hope the motion today will help draw attention to the plight of the Iraqi people and to some of the very credible reports which have been produced by the international community such as UNICEF, Doctors Without Borders and many others who have witnessed firsthand what has happened and have given evidence to their witness of that.

Another point I would like to make is the member from the Canadian Alliance made an outrageous statement that the Arab summit was not in favour of lifting the sanctions, which was absolutely not the case. That is totally false.

In fact, the Amman Declaration of March 28 from the 13th Arab summit, clearly stated:

We call for lifting the sanctions on Iraq and for dealing with the humanitarian issues pertaining to Iraq, Kuwaiti and other prisoners of war according to the principles of our religion and national heritage.

Therefore, the Alliance member was clearly false in his assertion.

In closing, I want to thank the member for Burnaby—Douglas for bringing forward this issue again; a sane idea, a saner policy for a humane world where we do not destroy a civil society because we are trying to get at one person.

I hope the members of this House will consider this motion and, like the local and national organizations who have worked so hard, put pressure on our Canadian government to convince it to be part of an effort to lift these sanctions.

Mr. Svend Robinson: Madam Speaker, in the final minutes of this debate I want to certainly thank my colleague, the member for Vancouver East, for once again eloquently speaking out for justice, for human rights, for the rights of the people of Iraq to live in dignity and in support of this motion for the lifting of sanctions. I also want to thank my colleague from Pictou—Antigonish—Guysborough for his very thoughtful comments.

I must say that I am really quite shocked at the fact that not a single Liberal member of parliament was prepared to stand during the course of this debate and speak out in support of what Liberal members voted in favour of during the last parliament. The foreign affairs committee in that last parliament passed a motion unanimously with the support of every party, including the Alliance Party and the Liberals. I see the parliamentary secretary here who was a member of that committee and voted in favour of this motion, as did the member for Esquimalt—Juan de Fuca. The motion passed unanimously stated:

Notwithstanding the adoption of security council resolution 1284, the committee urgently pursue the delinking of economic from military sanctions with a view to rapidly lifting economic sanctions in order to significantly improve the humanitarian situation of the Iraqi people.

That is what the motion today calls for. It is unbelievable that members who voted in favour of this principle in the last parliament now are condemning it. How many more innocent Iraqi lives have been lost over the course of just the last year?

They say we have to maintain these economic sanctions because of concern about weapons of mass destruction in Iraq. They ignore the report that they signed on to. In fact that report states very clearly, referring to a March 1999 report of the UN expert panel on disarmament "The bulk of Iraq's prescribed weapons programs have been eliminated—100% of verification may be an unattainable goal".

Indeed the former lead United Nations weapons inspector, Scott Ritter, has emphatically declared that Iraq was qualitatively disarmed of weapons of mass destruction from 1991 to 1998. Yet of course there was no lifting of sanctions.

I have no doubt that if the international community, with Canada leading in this, were to make it very clear to the Iraqi government that we were prepared to lift economic sanctions by a specific and firm date with international guarantees, Iraq would be prepared to allow the readmission of arms inspectors into that country and an assurance that any evidence of weapons that were being produced illegally would be dealt with and dealt with firmly. However, that is not what is happening here today.

I want to appeal to members once again to recognize the impact of this. The fact is that we as Canadians are spending some $35 million every year in enforcing these insane and genocidal sanctions. We have spent over $1 billion since 1991 in this region. I do not believe that Canadians who know of the impact of these sanctions on innocent human lives support this for one minute.

Dennis Halliday, the former United Nations humanitarian co-ordinator, in speaking of these sanctions said "We are destroying an entire society. It is as simple and as terrifying as that".

He is right. The purpose of this motion is to call for leadership. It is a tragic coincidence that we are debating this motion on the eve of Mother's Day. I recall so vividly meeting many Iraqi mothers who had lost children as a result of these sanctions. I recall looking into the eyes of an Iraqi mother who pleaded with me "Why are you killing my innocent child?" I could not answer that question.

I appeal on the eve of Mother's Day for the international community and Canada to show leadership to end the impact of these destructive and genocidal sanctions and ensure that no more children, no more innocent people in Iraq, die as a result of these sanctions. That is my plea. That was the unanimous plea of the Standing Committee on Foreign Affairs and International Trade in its report.

In closing, I seek unanimous consent of the House at this time that this motion might be made votable so at the very least the House could debate the issue and ensure that Canadians are given an opportunity to be heard in the committee on a profoundly important issue of life and death.

1 October, 2001: I write to Svend Robinson concerning the aftermath of September 11, 2001 terrorist attack on the World Trade Center. The media, including the Canadian media, has unleashed a hateful hysteria against Islam and Muslims.

21 November, 2001: Svend responds, "NDP leader Alexa McDonough and our federal caucus have taken a strong stand on terrorism. We were the only party to vote against the US led military attack and the only party to vote against Bill C-36 at second reading, the sweeping and dangerous 'anti-terrorism' bill. We have called upon the government to significantly increase CIDA (Canadian International Development Agency) and to respond to the humanitarian disaster facing Afghani people."

From: "Robinson, Svend - M.P." <Robinson.S@parl.gc.ca>
To: <m.javed@sympatico.ca>
Sent: Wednesday, November 21, 2001 11:15 AM
Subject: RE: Thanks and a suggestion
OTTAWA   PLEASE QUOTE FILE
NO: RW01-28743

November 20th, 2001

Dear Mr Javed,

Thank you for contacting me regarding the aftermath of the September 11th
terrorist attacks on New York and Washington. NDP leader Alexa McDonough and
our federal caucus have taken a strong stand on terrorism. We were the only
party to vote against the US led military attacks and the only party to vote
against Bill C-36 at second reading, the sweeping and dangerous
"anti-terrorism" bill. We have called upon the government to significantly
increase CIDA aid to respond to the humanitarian disaster facing the Afghani
people.

New Democrats have joined in calling for the perpetrators of the September
11 attacks to be brought to justice before an international tribunal for
these crimes against humanity. Canada should have acted under Article 35 of
the Charter to call for this, instead of marching in lockstep with the US
off to a war that is already creating new civilian casualties, and breeding
new martyrs. We also condemned the Liberals' contempt for Parliament in
refusing to allow an immediate debate and vote on the deployment of our
troops.

In the longer term we must work to eradicate the conditions from which
despair, violence, hatred and discord arise. Canada must play a leading role
in the search for justice and peace, not join in the destructive calls for
retaliation and revenge that can only lead to a new cycle of violence and
hopelessness.

Thank you once again for contacting me on this important issue.

Sincerely Yours,

Svend Robinson MP
Burnaby-Douglas

SJR/rw

-----Original Message-----
From: Naheed Javed [mailto:m.javed@sympatico.ca]
Sent: October 1, 2001 6:45 PM
To: Robins@parl.gc.ca
Subject: Thanks and a suggestion

Mr. Svend Robinson, MP

Dear Sir:

Thank you very much for sending me the copy of the May 10, 01 House of
Commons Debate concerning the 'Sanctions against Iraq' that you pursued.
This voice definitely echoed and flashed from the Commons but unfortunately

fell on the deaf ears and blind eyes of many Liberals and the Government in the Commons.

Now after Sept. 11, 01 as we all know, the media, including the Canadian media has unleashed a hateful hysteria against Islam, and kindled wild burning fires of hatred against Muslims. Questions do arise in the minds of all those who want to promote good and prevent evil?

Will it be possible to leash the Canadian media?
Will our government, at least now, open their deaf ears and blind eyes?
Do they have the will to restrain the media?
Has the NDP discussed the need to pursue this matter in the parliament and with the Government?
Will this voice again fell on the deaf ears and blind eyes of many Liberals and the Government in the Commons?

It might be worth pursuing - for truth ultimately wins!

Thanking you and with best regards,

Sincerely,

Mohammed Javed, P.Eng.

N.B.: Please feel free to forward this e-mail to Ms. Alexa McDonough or other party members. Thanks.

Please note that my address has changed as follows:

Mohammed Javed
40 Westpointe Cres.
Nepean, ON
K2G 5Y9
e-mail: m.javed@sympatico.ca

People for peace

Dear editor:

I would like to thank this newspaper for publishing a photo of the peace rally that was held in Halifax on Feb. 20 to protest Canada's involvement in a possible Gulf war.

However, I would like to point out that the paper seems to have failed, though it could be inadvertent, to provide any other coverage of the rally.

The rally was organized, peaceful, dignified, and echoed the noble cause of peace. The streets of Halifax reverberated with the loud and clear voices of truth: "We want peace," "Stop the killing of Iraqi children," "No blood for oil."

The rally, organized on short notice, attracted more than 300 people from all walks of life, irrespective of culture, race, religion or social status. As pointed out by keynote speaker Jamal Badawi at Grand Parade, the rally had a human agenda — not a leftist, rightest or centrist one.

Most Canadians love peace. Why not Canada?

Most humans love peace. Why not the world?

Most Americans love peace. Why not America?

Mohammed Javed, a rally organizer, Lower Sackville

Chronicle Herald/
Mail Star
27 February 1998

Burden of death

Dear editor:

My government, the government of 30 million peace-loving Canadians, the government of Liberals, the government of Lloyd Axworthy and Jean Chretien, parroting the U.S. government, supports the deadly UN sanctions that kill 200 innocent, starving, deprived, gloomy and pathetic Iraqi children every day and have left more than a million such children dead.

Would I or any of the millions of Canadians that include Mr. Axworthy and Mr. Chretien bear the burden of seeing their pet animal, let alone their own child, being cruelly starved to death? No, we would not bear that burden unless our hearts had been sealed and our souls were dead.

Will this government dare to tell the truth to the U.S. government, loudly and clearly, that Canada cannot bear the burden of death and destruction of innocent Iraqi children?

I apologize for my harsh language, but the words have come out of my heart. I am sure this would be the loud and clear voice of 30 million Canadians if only they knew the truth!

Mohammed Javed, Lower Sackville

The Chronicle Herald   The Mail Star

Tuesday, March 28, 2000

Cruelly punished

Dear editor:

It is early Friday morning in Halifax on April 21. The Chronicle-Herald portrays a large picture titled "For our sins." It also reports, in bold headlines, the shooting death of Patricia's pet dog. For sure, it devastates her tender, emotional nine-year-old girl because her innocent pet is not only dead, but has been cruelly shot dead.

Somewhere else, not very far away, on our own planet, in a place called Iraq, a million innocent children, pets of their parents, have died and continue to die because of the cruel UN sanctions dictated by the U.S. government and vigorously supported by our Canadian government. They devastate not one or two, but a million parents, because their innocent children have been cruelly punished to death.

Does this devastate Lloyd Axworthy and Jean Chretien, too? I do not know the answer to this question. What I do know is that recently Mr. Axworthy announced, "generously," a million-dollar humanitarian aid package to Iraq. Is it "blood money" at the rate of $1 per dead child, or is it an atonement for the sin? Will Mr. Axworthy answer this single million-dollar question honestly? If Canada had answered it rightly, if the U.S. had answered it rightly, a million children would not have perished pathetically! A million parents would not have been devastated! How sad!

Mohammed Javed, Lower Sackville

The Chronicle Herald   The Mail Star
Thursday, May 4, 2000

Mr Javed,

Your son showed me the letter you wrote to the editor.

Good ideas! I couldn't agree more.

It makes me sick to my stomach sometimes when people forget the value of human life. Media focus on animals is sad and needs to be corrected.

I often have discussions with my students about ignorance and what is truly important in life.

We will be reading and discussing your letter as a class!

— John Walker

4 May, 2000

Growing momentum

Dear editor:

Mohammed Javed's letter of May 4 was disturbing. Further to his comparison of Iraqi children to our pets, I have to wonder if a sanctions regime that killed 200 of our pets every day would have gone on for close to 10 years.

There is growing international momentum against the sanctions. Many are calling this genocide and some are asking Canada to account for its complicity. Javed mentions the $1 million of "charity" Lloyd Axworthy gave Iraq, but does not mention the $36 million we are spending enforcing the sanctions. For anyone proud to be a Canadian, it is painful to see that, on the whole, we are subservient to American policy goals, starving people rather than acting as peacekeepers.

I encourage people to visit the Web site http://www.chebucto.ns.ca/CommunitySupport/NSCEIS/
Daniel Haran, Halifax

The Mail-Star   The Chronicle-Herald
Monday, May 15, 2000

What a contrast!

Dear editor:

This year, during the first summer of the new millennium, Canada's East Coast will witness an impressive event when the tall ships that have already set sail on a challenging, adventurous and constructive run will arrive at the Port of Halifax.

This year, during the same first summer of the new millennium, Canada's West Coast will witness an obscure event when the mighty Canadian warship HMCS Calgary, flexing its muscles, will set sail on a non-challenging, non-adventurous and destructive run toward the Arabian Gulf. The mission is to continue to enforce the deadly,

10-year-old, Canadian-supported UN sanctions against Iraq. Yes, the same sanctions that kill 200 innocent Iraqi children every day.

The Tall Ships 2000 will celebrate the run of the millennium. What will Art Eggleton's Calgary celebrate? The murder of a million innocent Iraqi children? What a comparison! What a contrast! Are we the humanity of the new millennium?

Mohammed Javed, Lower Sackville

The Chronicle Herald, The Mail Star
Monday, May 22, 2000

Transgressions repaid

Dear editor:

Not very long ago, during the Gulf War against Iraq, the United States of America, along with its allies, used extensively a new generation of deadly weapons and ordnance coated with depleted uranium. Radioactive DU's effect lingers on and on for numerous centuries; cancer is definitely taking its toll in Iraq.

A million children have perished pathetically under the UN sanctions to pay Washington's price. To the mighty U.S., this is not alarming, but only "a hard choice, a price that is worth it."

Such tyranny stemming out of vanity, pride and intoxication of power transgresses the laws and limits set forth by nature (the Creator). But nature has its own way of dealing with such transgressions. Look at the empires that were once mighty — they have crumbled and vanished. Look at some mighty tyrants — if Pharaoh and Goliath were mighty, there came a Moses and a David! Look at the dinosaurs; they were mighty, too, but are extinct now! Did the dinosaurs transgress the law of nature and wreak havoc on the earth?

Mohammed Javed, Lower Sackville

The Chronicle Herald, The Mail Star
Wednesday, June 14, 2000

Starve the beetles

To the editor:

Deadly brown spruce longhorn beetles are destroying the bulk of fine spruce trees in Point Pleasant Park. The mayor is concerned that all of Nova Scotia could be destroyed. I could think of a solution. Have an embargo and place the park under siege. Nothing should reach the deadly beetles. Starve them to death. The mayor, for sure, would like to know how could we enforce such an embargo?

He would have to enlist the services of Jean Chretien & Co. (a no-liability company) comprising of Lloyd Axworthy and Art Eggleton. They possess the necessary qualifications and expertise in abundance in a fairly similar, but very large, field and have in fact vigorously supported and implemented a deadly U.S. imposed, UN embargo — the embargo of the millennium against Iraq that has killed not one or two but a million innocent Iraqi children. The children have pathetically perished and the beetles, too, will be gone forever.

Mohammed Javed
Lower Sackville

The Daily News
June 29, 2000, Thursday

Our Iraqi policies hurt children

To the editor:

In Canada, thanks to our glorious democracy, we cherish individual rights and are determined to uphold the rights of others. We are free to think what we want and say what we want. We are peace-loving and peacekeeping people.

In pursuit of peace, we sail across high seas and reach as far away as the Arabian Gulf. We participate actively in the UN sanctions against Iraq because as Foreign Affairs Minister Lloyd Axworthy has stated in a recent response to me, "Canada believes that there remain serious security concerns surrounding Iraq's pursuit of nuclear, chemical and biological weapons." On the other hand, the former UN weapons inspector Scott Ritter has time and again asserted, "Iraq has been disarmed to a level unprecedented in modern history." Also, "Iraq has no significant weapons of mass destruction and no means to produce them in meaningful quantities."

These assertions are in addition to the fact that in the Middle East alone there are countries that do possess significant weapons of mass destruction but are not under UN sanctions.

Is Axworthy's so-called security concern true? Would he be able to say what he wants to say when his sayings and deeds have facilitated the killing of a million innocent Iraqi children? Is he determined to uphold the rights of others?

Is he keeping peace? Is he glorifying our glorious democracy?

Mohammed Javed
Lower Sackville

The Daily News
Tuesday, July 4, 2000

No compassion

Dear editor:

Re: the June 29 front-page story "Owner to pursue case after pit bull mauled dog." I do sympathize with poor little Mookie, a Lhasa Apso, who suffered a gash on his neck and a puncture wound in his mouth when the "macho" pit bull attacked to avenge a possible insult when the little one perhaps barked.

Still, it would be a pity if the pit bull is destroyed. That will be a clear cruelty to animals, a cruelty to dogs which are loved so much, cared for so much. The pit bull is not an alien, but a dog. It deserves to be treated fairly and compassionately and trained to be non-violent. Our compas-

sionate value system does not permit the cruelty of destruction of living beings, be they destructive criminals, serial killers or violent dogs.

However, is it not sad that such a compassionate value system has been overruled by Lloyd Axworthy to bring forth the destruction of a million Iraqi children, by vigorously supporting the demon of U.S-imposed UN sanctions? The only difference: here, it is a question of destruction of a macho dog; there, it was the destruction of a million innocent children. The dog shall not be destroyed. The children should not have been destroyed.

Mohammed Javed, Lower Sackville

The Chronicle Herald The Mail Star
Monday, July 10, 2000

Crime against Iraq

Dear editor:

According to a recent report in this newspaper, Canada fully supports the formation of a permanent international criminal court of justice to deal with crimes against humanity.

Foreign Affairs Minister Lloyd Axworthy is keen to advance human security "by ensuring that those who have committed crimes against humanity do not escape justice."

For sure, the minister will have a unique distinction of being amongst the promoters of international criminal justice.

But the U.S. has so far refused to sign the statute to establish such a court, obviously because its crimes against humanity would not escape justice.

One such example is the mega crime of UN sanctions against Iraq, imposed by the United States, that have killed a million children there. Mr. Axworthy, too, has vigorously supported the sanctions.

But is he sure that the sanctions are not a crime against humanity, a crime against innocent children?

Let the pathetic screams of dying children tell the truth, and if they are right, will Mr. Axworthy be subject to the justice of his proposed court and retain the unique distinction of being amongst the promoters of international criminal justice?

Mohammed Javed, Lower Sackville

The Chronicle Herald   The Mail Star
Monday, July 24, 2000

Perfect flood next?

Dear editor:

Is it not alarming that Greenland's ice caps are melting at the rate of about 51 cubic kilometres annually, adding significantly to the rising sea level and increasing the risk of coastal flooding? The results of a recent NASA study, as reported by the journal Science, say so.

Noah's flood comes to mind. Will history repeat itself? Evil was at a peak then. Evil is substantial and sufficient now, at least on the part of Washington D.C., to qualify it for a flood. Since Aug. 6, a decade ago, it has wreaked unprecedented havoc and continues to do so in the bloodbath of innocent Iraqi children, under the guise of UN sanctions. Literally, the blood of a million innocent children would have flooded the Euphrates and Tigris. Incidentally or deliberately, Aug. 6 coincides with the dropping of the first atomic bombs on the civilians in Japan by the same Washington, D.C.

The setting for a perfect storm, a perfect flood, is evident, and Washington, D.C., is not far away from the sea. It seems that it is only a matter of time for the repeating of the overwhelming Noah's flood. The Halloween storm, a sample storm of 1991, has shown its fury with waves higher than 30 metres and causing billions of dollars in damage.

Will the evil doers of Washington, D.C., board the ark or seek a mountain to save themselves, rather than drown themselves?

Mohammed Javed, Lower Sackville

The Chronicle Herald The Mail Star
Sunday, August 6, 2000

No more floods

Dear editor:

I would like to reply to Mohammed Javed's letter, in the Aug. 6 Sunday Herald, about the world being destroyed again by a flood.

Would you please read the King James Bible, the Book of Genesis chapter 9, verses 11-17 and learn of the rainbow. It's a beautiful passage of God's promise. The world will not be destroyed by a flood again.

Ruby G. Heffler, Shelburne

The Chronicle Herald   The Mail Star
Sunday, August 20, 2000

Fires of war

Dear editor:

The full moon of mid-August, with its serene light, is a witness to scores of wildfires that are raging out of control in 13 Western states of the U.S.

The total area burned so far this year is about 4.5 million acres, three and a quarter times the size of Prince Edward Island. The U.S. is fighting a relentless, but losing battle to control the rage of roaring flames.

The full moon now, and scores of time since a decade, has also been a sad witness to something more dreadful. It is the death and destruction caused by fires brought forth by more than 140,000 tons of explosives, equivalent to about seven nuclear bombs that the U.S. (with allies) has dropped in its war, said to be against Saddam Hussein, but in reality against the people of Iraq.

The U.S. is continuing its game of fire by bombing on an average of once every two days. Every lunar month, the moon is yet a sad witness to the fast-expanding cemeteries, with 6,000 innocent dead children added, as a result of the cruel U.S.-imposed UN sanctions.

Wildfires will continue to rage till nature stops them. But will the U.S. stop playing with fire that it cannot contain? Has the U.S. begun to lose both the battle and the war? Could it be a victory when a million children have perished? What will the full moon of future witness?

Mohammed Javed, Lower Sackville

*The Chronicle Herald   The Mail Star
Monday, 21 August, 2000*

No tricks needed

Dear Editor:

Re: Ruby Heffler's letter "No more floods" (The Sunday Herald, Aug. 20).

Noah, the deluge, and God's (Allah's) "portent for the peoples" are discussed in the Holy Koran: Surah xxix: verses 14 and 15. The Christian and Jewish teachings are not the only places to find the "word of God."

Newton's demonstration of refraction of white light adequately explains the phenomenon of the rainbow, without the intervention of the Almighty! It turns out that it would be more impressive if the bow were extinguished during the brilliant sunshine and post-deluge condition. The talent of the ancients for attributing phenomena as messages from God is rivalled only by the ingenious propensity of "Bible thumpers" to enlarge upon it.

Better to go to Lamentations 3:22 and 23 for a message on His/Her mercy. Of course, the Good Book is full of texts similar to this, without conjuring tricks.

Bill Charlton, Port Hawkesbury

The Chronicle Herald   The Mail Star
Sunday, August 27, 2000

Battle weary?

Dear editor:

We excel in the art of peacekeeping and now our government wants to surpass in the art of war too, fighting determined battles and waging wars, winning some and losing others in the process.

Art Eggleton successfully challenged a rogue U.S. ship on the high seas, that was holding at ransom our military cargo, and brought it to its knees.

The "Battle of Beetles," which involves the destruction of brown spruce longhorn beetles, is raging in the federal courts. The government is insisting that it will not rest unless and until it chops off at least half of the 10,000 originally slated trees.

Blood has flowed in the pitched and unsettled battles of the "Fish War" in Miramichi.

In the "Battle of Pie," our undefended prime minister himself was shot with a pie. However, he has fought and won the "Battle of a Neck" by throttling a protester.

"War of Sanctions" is yet another war, a war against the people of Iraq. In pursuit of this war, our government — which is programmed to say "yes" to the U.S. — has sailed across high seas and reached the Persian Gulf and is part of the fleet that imposes UN sanctions. Will the government master the art of war when a million innocent children have perished pathetically?

Mohammed Javed, Lower Sackville

*The Chronicle Herald The Mail Star
Wednesday, September 6, 2000*

Not that worthy

Dear editor:

Your Sept. 21 editorial "Axworthy was worthy" glorifies him, saying: "Axworthy isn't just another brick in the Liberal wall. He is a cornerstone of our foreign policy. . . . Mr. Axworthy has made a difference in the government's soulless agenda."

Yes, he has not left even a single stone unturned in making a difference — be it positive or negative. But why did the editorial fail to see the other side of the coin, and not even mention that Axworthy pursued a foreign policy known as the Iraq policy?

This soulless agenda, in collusion with the U.S. in the guise of UN sanctions, has brought disaster to the people of Iraq.

Axworthy's pretext for pursuing such a policy was the so-called security concern emanating from Iraq. Former UN weapons inspector Scott Ritter has asserted Iraq has been disarmed to an unprecedented level. Egyptian Foreign Minister Amr Moussa says: "We and others see that after 10 years of sanctions and embargo, it is not possible for Iraq to be the threat that was present in 1990."

Axworthy boasts (in a June response to me) that during the April 2000 presidency of the UN Security Council, Canada announced the creation of a Security Council working group to recommend ways to improve the effectiveness of UN sanctions. Yes, they are highly "effective" — they kill 200 children a day!

Considering the other side of the coin, did Axworthy make a difference in reshaping government's soulless agenda to a soulful one? Was Axworthy worthy?

Mohammed Javed, Lower Sackville

The Chronicle Herald The Mail Star
Tuesday, 26 September, 2000

A line of captured Iraqi soldiers are marched through the desert in Kuwait, past a group of U.S. vehicles during the Gulf War. Ten years later, the war is far from over for Iraqi citizens and Gulf War veterans who may be victims of radiation poisoning from depleted uranium.

An undeclared nuclear war

By Mohammed Javed

THE GULF WAR was an undeclared nuclear war and continues to remain so. "New evidence" as reported by the Sunday Times (Sept. 3) indicates that "tens of thousands of British and American soldiers are dying from radiation."

They seem to have inhaled tiny uranium particles when more than 740,000 depleted uranium coated shells were fired nearly a decade ago. Every cruise missile which rains on Iraq every now and then contains DU.

The U.S. government admits having used 300 tons of DU during the war. Experts indicate some 700 tons of radioactive uranium dust is left in Iraq. Our Canadian uranium basically provides material for the horror weapons that are made in the "devil's workshop" in the U.S.

DU remains radioactive for 4,500 million years.

Dr. Asaf Durakovic, who is a life professor of nuclear medicine at Georgetown University Hospital, Washington, D.C. has tested the veterans and found "excess levels" of depleted uranium in 70 per cent of them, nearly a decade after the Gulf War. Excess uranium is normally flushed out, but surprisingly the veterans have re-

tained it.

DU causes slow death from cancers and kidney damage. Mr. Durakovic also says that DU is a leading contributing factor in the majority of those affected by Gulf War syndrome. News reports talk of secret American documents claiming that the U.S. army was aware that DU was potentially harmful, but the Pentagon says it is "only very very mildly radioactive."

Canadian scientist Dr. Rosalie Bertell, who is one of the world's leading authorities on health effects of low-level radiation, has tested some of the veterans here in Canada and has found DU in their urine at quite a high level, even after nearly a decade. She says inhaled DU keeps irradiating the tissue around it wherever it is in the body.

Professor Siegwart-Horst Guenther, founder of the Austrian Yellow Cross, took a Gulf War DU bullet encased in a lead-lined box to Germany for analysis. The bullet activated all radiation sensors at the airport and he was arrested.

As many as 4,500 Canadian soldiers served in the war and the possibility of radiation poisoning cannot be ruled out. The Department of National Defence, in a report issued in June 1998 based on an earlier study, coolly discounts the is-

sue of Gulf War Syndrome. "The study in fact finds that the conditions associated with Gulf War service could well be stress-induced. It finds that these same conditions exist in veterans of other deployments, but to a lesser extent than in Gulf War veterans."

The British government refuses to accept that the syndrome even exists. However, the U.K. Atomic Energy authority has said that 50 tonnes of residual dust left in an area of hostilities could cause half a million extra cancer deaths in a decade.

In the U.S., about 115,000 veterans have been diagnosed as having Gulf War Syndrome. But surprisingly, until June 1999, none had been tested for DU.

More than 1.2 million people, including about one million innocent children, have so far perished in Iraq, as a result of war and sanctions. Radiation has already begun to kill and will continue to kill for centuries to come.

The BBC has reported that Gulf War shells could be causing children's cancers and says, "High numbers of children born with cancer in the areas of Iraq where the Gulf War was fought have increased fears that the weapons used by Allies may be responsible."

Abnormalities, as well as

cancers including leukemia and mutations, have increased dramatically. Children are born without eyes or limbs. Pictures show how children lie in terrible pain, bleeding internally, covered in bruises from leaking capillaries, bloated with oedema, eyes full of unshed tears. A soulful and kind-hearted Westerner who visited the remains of a hospital in Iraq, bent up to stroke such a child's face, said "the child's hand came up and grabbed mine and squeezed it with all its might, a gesture of trust, pleading and spontaneity. I left the ward, leaned against a wall and prayed for the ground to open and swallow me up."

But what has happened to the heart and soul of Bush (senior), Major, Clinton, Albright, Blair, Chretien, Axworthy and others? The new stalwart in the continuing war will be Gore or Bush.

For the veterans, the war has ended, but not their battle with radiation. For 22 million people of Iraq, the war — the undeclared nuclear war, the radiation, the sanctions, the low-profile bombings, the propaganda — has not ended. The innocent will have to continue their struggle against the official U.S. evil for centuries to come!

Mohammed Javed, P.Eng., lives in Sackville, N.S.

The Chronicle Herald The Mail Star
Saturday, September 30, 2000

Must be condemned

Dear editor:

The Sept. 30 opinion article by Mohammed Javed, about the continuing ravaging war against the people of Iraq, is compelling and accurate.

The initial attack on Iraq in 1991 by the U.S. and its allies, destroying its infrastructure and using depleted uranium, brought death and disease to Iraq's children and civilian population, as well as to U.S. veterans and our own veterans. There is scientific evidence that the use of depleted uranium has caused, since 1991, a fourfold increase of cancer and leukemia among Iraqi children. This has not spared the unborn, where congenital abnormalities are rife. The use of DU contravenes the UN charter.

This action is compounded by the continuing infliction of economic sanctions, which has brought about disease and starvation among the people of Iraq. About 5,000 children under age five die every month due to these sanctions.

Ramsey Clark, the former attorney general of the U.S., described these as "genocidal sanctions." Denis Halliday, assistant UN secretary-general and UN humanitarian co-ordinator in Iraq, resigned his post in September 1998 in disgust at this systematic killing.

The U.S. and Britain, in continuing these sanctions against the innocent people of Iraq, assisted by the support of our government, are committing war crimes that must be condemned by all who have a sense of humanity.

Ismail Zayid, MD, Halifax

The Chronicle Herald   The Mail Star
Wednesday, October 11, 2000

Dare to care

Dear editor:

Imagine a Canadian humanitarian mission flying to Baghdad after more than a decade of the cruel U.S.-imposed UN sanctions on Iraq, that include an embargo on flights too. The recent Russian, French and British flights "committed" a "blatant violation" of the sanctions regime when they flew to Baghdad, defying the ban.

Such a mission, "Canadians to Baghdad," is not just a thought now. A dedicated group of Canadians named Nova Scotia Campaign to End Iraq Sanctions, who feel the agony of innocent children dying at an alarming rate of 200 per day, have written to the UN Secretary General. They have written, on behalf of all peace-loving Canadians (excluding the soulless government of Jean Chretien), that they are concerned about the devastating impact of sanctions and asking permission for their intended flight to Baghdad that will carry goodwill ambassadors, food, humanitarian and medical relief supplies.

When in Baghdad, they want to tell the dying children, "We care for you. We love you and we are not among those murderers who shamelessly say that it is worth the price." They want to tell the Canadian government, the U.S. government, the UN, the world and, above all, the innocent children that they dare to care.

Yes, the Canadians dare to care, but will the U.S., where democracy is in a state of utter confusion, still call the humanitarian mission a "blatant violation" of the sanctions regime?

Mohammed Javed, Lower Sackville

The Chronicle Herald The Mail Star Tuesday, November 28, 2000

No justification

Dear editor:

It is January 2001. It is the birth month of humane Aquarians; but Melanie the cat was killed mercilessly after a veterinarian who feared for his safety bashed it against a concrete floor not once, but twice. It is the 10th anniversary of the Gulf War, too, and more than a decade has passed since the sanctions have been imposed on Iraq.

Your editorial writer thought it apt to commemorate the occasion of the 10th anniversary of the Gulf War and wrote an editorial titled "Iraqi impasse" (Jan. 19). He did mention the death of thousands, and the deaths that are continuing, and wrote: "Humanitarian groups say that is because the United States, backed by the UN, continues to prosecute a needless war against Iraq. We hold a contrary view. It is Iraq which continues to prosecute a needless war against the international community."

Many of your humane readers did not believe the veterinarian's justification for killing mercilessly a harmless and innocent cat just out of fear of it.

Not one or two, but a million harmless and innocent children have perished due to the cruel sanctions. Will your humane readers believe the justification to have killed them mercilessly out of fear of "Melanie the Cat" or "Winnie the Pooh?"

Mohammed Javed, Lower Sackville

The Chronicle Herald The Mail Star
Saturday, January 27, 2001

Unending drama

Dear editor:

The act in the decade-old drama is too familiar: U.S and British planes have again bombed Iraq. This time, the new macho "cowboy from Texas" sent a new "unmistakable message" to the "demon of Iraq," 10 years after the dad, "the elder cowboy," sent it massively in the "Desert Storm."

The laser-accurate bombs always do reach their destination, but the "unmistakable messages" never do so. Unfortunately, in the merry-go-round of the unending drama, the bombing continues, and the cruel sanctions remain well in place. A million innocent children have perished, but the familiar acts in the drama have survived.

The cowboy from Texas, seemingly unable to withstand the cold weather of Washington, D.C., broke tradition, and made his first foreign trip to Mexico instead of to Canada. There, in sunny Mexico, he flexed his muscles and unleashed his guns on Iraq.

I wish the president had made his first foreign trip to Ottawa. Then, would the lack of sunshine, the snow, and the cold weather have dampened his spirit to reach out for his guns? It might have at least delayed the familiar act of the drama.

Mohammed Javed, Lower Sackville

The Chronicle Herald The Mail Star
February 26, 2001

5 August, 2013: I write to Svend Robinson after a long time, in 2013. I receive a reply immediately from him. The following trail of emails describes the details of actions that he undertook beyond November 2001 with regards to the sanctions.

From: mohammed_javed48@hotmail.com
To: svend@svendrobinson.com
Subject: Your work to lift the sanctions
Date: Mon, 5 Aug 2013 06:14:23 -0700

Dear Svend Robinson,

Good morning. Hope you would recall that I was in touch with you concerning Iraq sanctions during 1999 and 2000, when you as a MP, were dedicated in your efforts to bring an end to the inhuman sanctions that were taking the lives of about 200 children per day.

The correspondence with you has been informative and quite encouraging, and I have retained it.

I have started thinking about writing a book and its possible contents may contain:

1. Correspondence with Svend Robinson, MP; the then prime minister of Canada; Foreign Affairs Minister (Axworthy); Art Eggleton (Defence Minister); Bill Grahm, MP and chair SCFAIT; Peter Stoffer, MP, etc.
2. Hearings of SCFAIT, House of Commons debates, House of Commons Report, and Recommendation. Softening of Canada's stand on sanctions.
3. Reproduce some of my published letters and articles about Iraq (from *Chronicle Herald* of Halifax).
4. Humanitarian flight proposal to Iraq.

I have met you a couple of times, though briefly, once in Halifax, and then during a dinner at Parliament Hill.

Looking forward to hear from you about your thoughts on this matter.

With best regards,
Mohammed Javed

P.S: Presently I am working as Chairperson of I-LEAD Conference (ileadottawa.ca)

From: sjr99@hotmail.com
To: mohammed_javed48@hotmail.com
Subject: RE: Your work to lift the sanctions
Date: Mon, 5 Aug 2013 19:50:36 +0000

Dear Mr Javed

Good to hear from you.

Your proposed book does sound like a good idea, please do feel free to share our correspondence from that time.

All the best with your project, I look forward to reading the book when completed!

Svend

From: mohammed_javed48@hotmail.com
To: sjr99@hotmail.com
Subject: RE: Your work to lift the sanctions
Date: Mon, 5 Aug 2013 16:22:31 -0700

Hi Svend,

Appreciate your prompt response and the go ahead from you to share the correspondence from that time – it would certainly be essential and important.

I would be taking the liberty to contact you to get further information as needed. I think something like an introduction or foreword by you would be valuable.

Yet, I don't have a timeline to complete the proposed book. It would certainly be my pleasure to send, not only the completed book to you but the draft too – for your valuable suggestions and comments!

With best regards,
Mohammed Javed

From: mohammed_javed48@hotmail.com
To: sjr99@hotmail.com
Subject: RE: Your work to lift the sanctions
Date: Sun, 9 Mar 2014 14:26:50 -0700

Dear Svend,

Good afternoon. This is further to our correspondence dated 5 August 2013 about the proposed book on Iraq sanctions.

I have prepared the first rough draft of the proposed book about the sanctions, and as previously indicated the contents include:

- Correspondence with you and others which include, the then Prime Minister of Canada (Jean Chrétien); Foreign Affairs Minister (Lloyd Axworthy); Defence Minister (Art Eggleton); Chair SCFAIT (Bill Grahm), etc. I have also included my comments on the correspondence.

- Hearings of SCFAIT, House of Commons Debates, House of Commons Report and Recommendation.
- Humanitarian flight proposal to Iraq.
- Have reproduced some of my published letters and articles about Iraq (from *Chronicle Herald, Mail Star* of Halifax, and *Daily News*).

May I request you to look into and help me with the following:

1. The contents certainly highlight your untiring efforts in the House of Commons to lift the sanctions. The book would be a tribute to your efforts and that of the NDP.

2. My correspondence with you and others in the then Liberal Government ends as of November 2001, beyond that I have no idea of what happened in the House of Commons, and how your efforts to end the sanctions materialized. The sanctions continued till 22 May 2003, and ended after the second Gulf War. I am sure that efforts of dedicated people like you would have eased the sanctions and saved numerous innocent lives from being further eliminated mercilessly. May I take the liberty to suggest that you add a concluding chapter to the book to include your efforts and that of NDP.

3. I would certainly appreciate your comments, and valuable suggestions with regards to the book including its improvement and publication.

Appreciate your cooperation and looking forward to hear from you at your earliest please.

Mohammed Javed

From: mohammed_javed48@hotmail.com
To: sjr99@hotmail.com
Subject: RE: Your work to lift the sanctions
Date: Mon, 10 Mar 2014 15:36:25 -0700

Dear Svend,

Nice to hear from you and that too so promptly, and your encouragement to pursue this 'important' book is certainly significant and important. I appreciate your recalling of the actions that you undertook beyond November 2001 – these along with our new correspondence could be added to the concluding chapter of the book. I am sure that you would permit such use. I would keep you posted.

   I would certainly be interested in reading your bio written by Graeme Truelove.

With best regards,
Mohammed Javed

From: sjr99@hotmail.com
To: mohammed_javed48@hotmail.com
Subject: RE: Your work to lift the sanctions
Date: Mon, 10 Mar 2014 20:44:07 +0000

Dear Mohammed

Good to hear from you, and I am glad to hear that the Iraq book is coming along well. In terms of actions I undertook post-November 2001, I recall a couple in particular. I spoke at a conference in Baghdad in May of 2002, and then several times afterwards in Canada, including a big gathering of over 1000 people in Vancouver in October 2002 when Scott Ritter and I spoke:

OCTOBER 4, 2002, VANCOUVER: A former United Nations Chief Weapons Inspector in Iraq, Scott Ritter spoke to over 1100 people at the First Baptist Church in Vancouver and exposed the lie to White House justifications for its new war against Iraq, (commenced in March 2003).

"There is no case for war. It would not be justified in international law and it would be morally wrong,"

Ritter told a cheering audience which packed the church. Organizers counted over 500 people lined up outside who weren't able to get in. Some who couldn't find a seat hung from open windows to hear Ritter speak.

Svend Robinson, Member of Parliament for Burnaby-Douglas also spoke and praised Ritter for his courage and determination to stop the war. Robinson, the NDP Foreign Affairs Critic in Parliament, has also spoken out recently against the Canadian government's complicity in the American campaign which he said is, "really about controlling oil interests in the Middle East, and not about any threat from weapons of mass destruction".

Below is a copy of my speech from the Baghdad conference....

Afraid I do not have time to write a contribution or read the draft, but I very much look forward to seeing the book. Have you had a chance to read the bio that was recently published about my life in politics ... you can find it on Amazon, author is Graeme Truelove. You would enjoy it.

Good luck with this important book!

Best
Svend

Svend at Baghdad Conference
7 May 2002

I would like to thank organizers of this conference for the honour and privilege of participating, and for being invited to say a few words on behalf of the Canadian delegation to the conference. I want to pay special tribute to my colleague George Galloway, the British MP for his tireless, dedicated commitment to the people of Iraq. He has travelled around the world, including my own country Canada, to lift his eloquent voice against the genocidal sanctions ... thank you George, for your courageous leadership. I would like to pay special tribute to Myriam and all of the children of Iraq.

This is my third visit to Iraq. The first was in the fall of 1990, when I led a Parliamentary delegation from Canada to speak out for peace, and oppose a military assault on Iraq. La dernière fois, j'ai participé dans une délégation du groupe Québécois, *Objection de Conscience*, en janvier 2000. Nous avons visité Baghdad et Basra, et nous avons observé les résultats dévastateurs des sanctions économiques, des bombardements, de l'uranium appauvri, de la destruction de l'infrastructure du pays.

Following my visit in 2000, the Canadian Parliamentary Foreign Affairs Committee held public hearings which led to a unanimous, all party report that recommended the lifting of economic sanctions and the re-establishment of a diplomatic presence in Iraq. The Chair of that Committee is now the Foreign Minister of Canada, Bill Graham.

I am back again in Iraq, together with my colleagues from Canada, to once again speak out against the inhumane sanctions, the illegal bombing, and to join my voice with those from people around the world in demand that the United States do not extend its immoral and illegal "war against terrorism" to the people of Iraq, who have already suffered too much. This "war", which has led to the brutal suppression of basic human rights and international humanitarian law, and the death of over 4000 innocent Afghan civilians, not to mention innocent Canadian soldiers killed by the US "friendly fire", must not be extended to Iraq. The US must not be allowed to inflict further terror and violence on the people of Iraq. The lives of Iraqi children are just as precious as the lives of the innocent civilians who perished in the World Trade Center. The Canadian Prime Minister, during a meeting in February with Russian President Putin, stated that Canada will not support a US led war on Iraq without UN authority, and in saying that he reflects the widely held views of the Canadian people. I urge the Iraqi government to give serious consideration to accepting the proposal of the Russian government to re-admit UN weapons inspectors to Iraq, subject of course to assurances that they are completely impartial and neutral, and lift economic sanctions within 60 days thereafter. Canadians in growing numbers, in the national organization CANESI, Canadian Network to End Sanctions on Iraq, with representatives from churches, labour, doctors, academics, human rights groups, artists, du Quebec et de partout au Canada, are joining the anti-sanctions, anti-war movement.

We are also here today to join in calling for peace and justice for our brothers and sisters in Palestine, at this time of such pain and tragedy. Two weeks ago I travelled to Jerusalem and the outskirts of Ramallah, as well as to Tel Aviv. I was blocked from meeting President Arafat, but I visited Qalandiya refugee camp, and heard eyewitness stories of the most appalling brutality, humiliation, torture and murder by the Israeli army. Those who are responsible for terrible war crimes, whether the killings at Sabra and Chatilla or the gassings of Kurds at Halabja, must be brought to justice. It is time that the international community stopped shamefully surrendering to the Israeli government's refusal to allow a UN inquiry into the horrors of Jenin. The UN should send the inquiry at once, and further should immediately send an International Protection Force to the occupied territories. Israel must respect the 4th Geneva Convention, and withdraw from all territories occupied since 1967, dismantle illegal settlements, and respect the rights of Palestinian refugees under international law.

At the same time, I call upon the Iraqi government and President Saddam Hussein to respect the right of Israel to exist within secure pre 1967 borders, and to stop glorifying the suicide bombers who take the lives of innocent Israeli citizens, both Arab and Jew. While we all understand the despair, the anguish and hopelessness of those who live in the squalid refugee camps, nothing, I repeat nothing can justify the mass murder of innocent people who are out at a discotheque or a restaurant or celebrating a religious holiday.

In closing, let me again pay tribute to the people of Iraq, the proud, dignified people who have suffered such tragedy at the hands of the US, the UK, and too many other countries including my own. The world will, I am convinced, look back on these terrible crimes with shock and revulsion and ask how this evil could have happened. We must break the silence and speak out in our own countries and demand that this genocide end. The people of Iraq alone must have the right to freely determine their future, not George Bush, not Tony Blair or any other world leader. And yes, I do look forward to the day when the brave people of Iraq are able to live in a country that is not subject to these inhumane sanctions and bombing. I look forward as well to the day when the people of Iraq are able to live in a democratic society that respects the fundamental human rights of all of its citizens; - that does not brutally repress all political dissent, that respects religious and cultural diversity and the rights of all minorities including the Kurds in the north and the population in the southern marsh areas; - that rejects the mindless racism, anti-semitism and xenophobia of the Jean Marie LePens and Jorg Haiders of this world; - that ensures full equality for women in all aspects of society; - that treats homosexuals such as myself with full dignity and respect instead of inhumanely using religion as an excuse to persecute and imprison them;- that respects freedom of the press, and whose leaders are revered and honoured for their wisdom and integrity, who need no portraits or monuments or palaces or extravagant birthday celebrations to earn the love of their people.

The people of Iraq have suffered long enough. End the sanctions, stop the bombing, respect human rights and let these proud people live in peace and harmony in this beautiful country of Iraq.

Thank you, Merci, Shokran

CHAPTER 6
SANCTIONS, MIDDLE EAST WARS, RISE OF TERRORISM, RISE OF ISLAMOPHOBIA

"Allah does not forbid you from those who do not fight you
because of religion and do not expel you from your homes –
from being righteous toward them and acting justly toward them.
Indeed, Allah loves those who act justly."
—*The Holy Qur'an 60:8*

The First Gulf War of 1991, the Iraq sanctions, followed by the Second Gulf War in Iraq, as well as the other American wars in the Middle East gave rise to terrorism and Islamophobia.

It may be worth mentioning President Bush Jr.'s keenness with the Second Gulf War. According to Bob Woodward, Bush told key Republicans in late 2005 that he would not withdraw from Iraq, "even if Laura (first Lady) and Barney (first dog) are the only ones supporting me." Bush Jr. went to war in Iraq claiming the so-called threat posed by Saddam Hussein's non-existent Weapons of Mass Destruction (WMDs) and also Hussein's so-called support for Al-Qaeda.

In February 2007, David Petraeus was appointed by President George W. Bush as the new US commander in Iraq. Petraeus oversaw the "surge" of 30,000 troops that President Bush had ordered in Iraq.

Ray McGovern, in an article describes that the surge "was misrepresented in the corporate media as a huge victory – because it was credited with a brief dip in the level of violence at the cost of some 1,000 American lives (and those of many more Iraqis) – but the 'surge' failed its principal goal of buying time to heal the rift between Shiites and Sunnis, a division that ultimately led to the emergence of the Islamic State (or ISIS)."[9]

McGovern points out that the Iraqi troops that were claimed to have been trained by Petraeus literally ran away from Mosul when attacked by the Islamic State's jihadists and left behind powerful US provided weapons for them to play with.

According to McGovern, Petraeus was instrumental in facilitating the emergence of the Islamic State by his policy of co-opting some Sunni tribes with promises of shared power in Baghdad and through bribes. He failed to fulfill his promises when the U.S.-installed Shia government in Baghdad did not comply with what had been promised.

McGovern further explains, "With huge sums of U.S. cash going to Sunni tribes in Anbar province, Al-Qaeda in Iraq just pulled back and regrouped. Its top leaders came from the ranks of angry Sunnis who had been officers in Saddam Hussein's army and – when the 'surge' failed to achieve reconciliation between Sunnis and Shiites – the U.S. cash proved useful in expanding Sunni resistance to Baghdad's Shiite government. From the failed 'surge' strategy emerged the rebranded Al-Qaeda in Iraq – the Islamic State."

McGovern also explains that, "The mess was made worse by subsequent U.S. strategy – beginning under Bush (Jr.) and expanding under President Obama – of supporting insurgents in Syria. By supplying money, guns and rockets to 'moderate' Sunni rebels, that strategy has allowed the materiel to quickly fall into the hands of Al-Qaeda's Syrian affiliate, Nusra Front, and its jihadist allies, Ahrar al-Sham. All this is among the fateful consequences of the U.S.-led invasion of Iraq 13 years ago – made worse (not better) by the 'surge' in 2007, which contributed significantly to this decade's Sunni-Shia violence. The real reason for Bush's 'surge' seems to have been to buy time so that he and Vice President, Dick Cheney could leave office without having a lost war on their résumés.

Patrick Cockburn, in an article wrote that President Trump will ignite a war with Iran, which will be great news for ISIS. He pointed out that:

> Of the three US presidents badly or terminally damaged by crisis in the Middle East, Jimmy Carter was the most unlucky, as there was nothing much he could do to stop the Iranian Revolution in 1979 or the seizure of diplomats in the US embassy in Tehran as hostages. Ronald Reagan's presidency saw military intervention in Lebanon where 241 US Marines were blown up in 1983, and the Iran-Contra scandal that permanently weakened the administration. Significant though these disasters and misadventures seemed at the time, none had the impact of George W Bush's invasion of Iraq in 2003 which led to the regeneration of al-Qaeda and the spread of chaos through the region.[10]

Cockburn further points out that, "Trump continually promised during the presidential election that he would focus exclusively in the Middle East on destroying ISIS, but one of the first moves of his administration has been to shift the US closer to Saudi Arabia by backing its war in Yemen. In his first statement of policy, Secretary of Defense James Mattis said that Iran is "the single biggest state sponsor of terrorism in the world." He explains that, "This is all good news for ISIS, though it has so many enemies committed to its defeat that a switch in US policy may be too late to do it a lot of good. But its main enemies on the ground are the Iraqi and Syrian armies, whose governments are backed by Iran, and the Syrian Kurds who fear that the US may soon give them less support in order to appease Turkey."

Patrick Cockburn, however, does not foresee a war with Iran in the immediate future. He predicts it after a year or two when the Iran policies of former President Obama run their course.

With regards to fighting terrorism, Mike Whitney, in an article, pointed out that former Vice President Joe Biden said, "Our biggest problem is our allies who are engaged in a proxy Sunni-Shiite war against Syrian President Bashar Assad. He specifically named Turkey, Saudi Arabia and the UAE. What did they do? They poured hundreds of millions of dollars and thousands of tons of weapons into anyone who would fight against Assad – except that the people who were being supplied were (Jabhat) Al-Nusra and Al-Qaeda and the extremist elements of jihadis coming from other parts of the world."[11] Joe Biden was later forced to apologize to UAE and Turkey over his remarks on Syria.

In May 2017, a suicide bomber Salman Abedi blew himself up at a packed Ariana Grande concert in Manchester, England. Twenty two people were killed. Jim Kavanagh wrote in his article that the Manchester bomber is the spawn of President Obama's and Secretary of State Hillary Clinton's policies in Libya.[12] Kavanagh pointed that:

Salman grew up in an anti-Qaddafi Libyan immigrant family. In 2011, his father, Ramadan Abedi, along with other British Libyans (including one who was under house arrest), "was allowed to go [to Libya], no questions asked," to join the Libyan Islamic Fighting Group (LIFG), an Al-Qaeda affiliate, to help overthrow Qaddafi. In Manchester, as Max Blumenthal puts it, in his excellent *Alternet* piece, it was all "part of the rat line operated by the MI5, which hustled anti-Qaddafi Libyan exiles to the front lines of the war." In Manchester, Salman lived near a number of LIFG militants, including an expert bomb maker. This was a tough bunch, and everybody—including the cops and Salman's Muslim neighbours—knew they weren't the Jets and the Sharks. As Middle East Eye reported, he "was known to security services," and some of his acquaintances "had reported him to the police via an anti-terrorism hotline."

CHAPTER 7
ISLAMOPHOBIA: INCIDENTS, CAUSES, STATISTICS, & PREDICTIONS

"And whatever good you put forward for yourselves – you will find it with Allah. It is better and greater in reward. And seek forgiveness of Allah. Indeed, Allah is Forgiving and Merciful."
—The Holy Qur'an 73:20

Donald Trump is not the first American politician to use anti-immigrant paranoia and Islamophobia for his political advantage. Islamophobia is defined as "dislike of or prejudice against Islam or Muslims, especially as a political force."

Lowell Flanders explains in his article:

> The campaign against Sharia by Mr. Gingrich, and some of the more obsessed acolytes of the neocon lobby, is just one aspect of an anti-Islamic campaign that threatens the rights and safety of American Muslims. The anti-Sharia gambit has been over-shadowed, however, by the acts of extremist violence in France, San Bernardino, Orlando, and more recently in New York, as the basis on which Islamophobia can be propagated. It is not difficult for an opportunistic politician to take advantage of the natural insecurity and fear provoked by these violent acts to

convince a worried public that he has all the answers. It just requires us to click our heels together three times and repeat the words 'radical Islamic extremism,' and the whole problem will disappear.[13]

Flanders wrote that according to George W. Bush, Al-Qaeda terrorists "hate our freedoms — our freedom of religion, our freedom of speech, our freedom to vote and assemble and disagree with each other." But Bush was careful not to equate the terrorists with all other Muslims. After 9/11, the Bush administration was able to curtail anti-Muslim sentiment to some extent. Flanders continued, "We also became involved in two wars that tended to focus attention on conflicts overseas rather than internal tensions here at home. Although there was distrust and suspicion of Muslims throughout this period, it has recently become more virulent. According to a study from the Center for Muslim-Christian Understanding at Georgetown University, anti-Muslim hate crimes increased in 2015, coinciding with attacks in Paris and San Bernardino, California, and the rise of Donald Trump, the GOP nominee for president who has called for intensified scrutiny of Muslims entering the United States."

Flanders quoted James Nolan, a former F.B.I. crime analyst, who stated that "there is a real spike in hate crimes against American Muslims which is caused in part by political candidates' raising the specter that radical Islam is at our doorstep." Flanders also quotes Mark Potok, a senior fellow at the Southern Poverty Law Center, which monitors hate groups and extremism, "I don't have the slightest doubt that Trump's campaign rhetoric has played a big part in the rising attacks."

Flanders pointed out that, "In the case of Muslims, Trump may increase the number of bureaucratic hoops they have to jump through to get into the country, and even extract a pledge of love from new immigrants. In a kind of reverse image of what Bush said after 9/11, Trump insists they must "love our freedoms — our freedom of religion, our freedom of speech, our freedom to vote and assemble and disagree with each other." But none of that will really address the issue of violence and terrorism in America, most of which has been committed by born-in-the-USA Americans. Between 1982 and 2016, out of 83 mass shootings or acts of terror, an immigrant committed only one; white people born here committed 48."

Andrew Levine, author and professor at the University of Wisconsin-Madison, said, "Bush did incalculable harm to the United States. Worse still, his wars – all of them wars of choice — destabilized large swathes of the Muslim world. It could take decades to put back together all that he broke, even if all goes well. Meanwhile, the consequences reverberate around the world."[14]

In January 2017, President Trump signed an executive order enacting a temporary suspension of all visas for nationals from Iraq, Iran, Libya, Somalia, Sudan, Syria, and Yemen. Alex Nowrasteh, an immigration policy analyst at the Cato Institute's Center for Global Liberty and Prosperity notes that "Foreigners from those seven nations have killed zero Americans in terrorist attacks on U.S. soil between 1975 and the end of 2015. Six Iranians, six Sudanese, two Somalis, two Iraqis, and one Yemini have been convicted of attempting or carrying out terrorist attacks on U.S. soil. Zero Libyans or Syrians have been convicted of planning a terrorist attack on U.S. soil during that time period."

Andrew Levine explained that Trump's Muslim travel ban makes Americans unsafe by giving credence to ISIS and other radical groups that the West is waging a war with the Muslim world. He points out that, "Since even before 9/11, our leaders have taken it upon themselves to encourage that fear (radical Islamic terrorism) – a complicated business in view of the close political and economic ties between the Muslim world and the West."

Canada is not free from this bias against Muslims. In a December 2016, opinion poll by Forum Research, among Canadian adults, 4-in-10 expressed some level of bias, or unfavourable feelings, against identifiable racial groups (41%), with Muslims having the highest negative rating (28%).[15] In a yet-to-be-published survey, ordered by the Quebec Human Rights Commission and reported by the *Montreal Gazette*, nearly half of Quebecers have an "unfavourable" view of religion. But this intolerance is unevenly split: while only 5.5 per cent of Quebecers expressed their dislike for the Christian cross, 48.9 per cent said they were uncomfortable with Muslim veils.[16]

According to a 2016 Environics poll, "One-third of Muslims in Canada have experienced discrimination or unfair treatment in the past five years due to their religion, ethnicity/culture, language, or sex. Such treatment is most commonly experienced in the workplace, public spaces, retail establishments and schools or universities." [17]

On 29 January, 2017, a lone gunman opened fire in a mosque in Quebec City, killing six people and injuring 19 others. He was known online for making statements inspired by extreme right-wing French nationalists. Jasmine Zine, a professor at Wilfrid Laurier University, pointed out in an article[18] that the "current breeding ground for Islamophobic hate is rooted in Canadian policies, practices, and the rhetoric of right wing politicians. The *Barbaric Cultural Practices Act* and proposal for a corresponding "tip line" by Conservative MP Kellie Leitch, Bill C-51/Anti-Terrorism Act, Security Certificates, as well as Bill 94, which sought to ban the niqab in Quebec and is now enforced through the Quebec Charter of Values (Bill 60) are among the policies that have cast Muslims as potential threats to national security and as illiberal and antithetical to 'Canadian values.'"

Zine quoted Haroun Bouazzi, co-president of the Montreal-based rights group AMAL-Quebec, "Mosques have been set ablaze and vandalized, and schools and halal butcher shops have been shot at, but in many instances, police have not labelled the attacks hate crimes." She pointed out that even though Canada has strong anti-hate laws, the lax enforcements leads to hate crimes going unreported or not prosecuted as hate crimes. She highlighted that police confirmed there were 14 reports of hate crimes in Montreal in the one week period after the Quebec City mosque shooting. She points out that across Canada hate crimes targeting Muslims have doubled between 2012 and 2014, even though overall hate crimes were down during the same period.

Zine said, "Fear and moral panic of 'radical jihadist youth' in the 'home grown' war on terror coupled with the idea that foreigners are changing the cultural landscape of Canada with their illiberal demands and strange barbaric customs create the ideological backdrop for the security state and the profiling of Muslims as potential threats to the nation. While Donald Trump has authorized and legitimized these views south of the border, similar ideas were already being promoted by Canada's former Prime Minister Stephen Harper."

Harper identified mosques as potential sites of radicalization. He said, "It doesn't matter what the age of the person is, or whether they're in a basement, or whether they're in a mosque or somewhere else." According to Zine, "such comparison is bound to linger in public thinking, given the Orientalist imagery produced in film, literature, and pop culture and now backed by a thriving Islamophobia industry that is gathering acceptance and momentum. Such hate-mongering about Muslims is gaining credence, which is wrongly being promoted by extreme right-wing politicians to project fear of terrorism as a Muslim threat."

Zine explained that "the actual shooter, Alexandre Bissonette a 24-year-old white male student from Université Laval with troubled ideological views will no doubt be cast as a solitary deviant whose crime has no bearing on his race or religion." She pointed out that:

White supremacists and anti-Immigrant groups are gaining traction in Canada. At least 100 right-wing extremist groups have been active in recent years including Golden Dawn, Sons of Odin, and Pegida. They are concentrated in Quebec, Western Ontario, Alberta, and British Columbia. While some members have engaged in random acts of violence, others have carried out targeted attacks on Muslims, Jews, people of colour, aboriginals and LGBTQ people. The Canadian Security Intelligence Service (CSIS) has acknowledged the presence of right-wing extremists, but they do not appear to be regarded as a high priority or threat. According to a CSIS spokesperson: "Right-wing extremist circles appear to be fragmented and primarily pose a threat to public order and not to national security." And yet in late 2014, a lieutenant from the Sûreté du Québec division that investigates domestic terrorism told a parliamentary committee, "a

> majority of the service's active files deal with the extreme right." Social media foments virtual spaces for radical right-wing extremists find solidarity and support. Sub-forums of the white supremacist website, Stormfront. org, are among the most popular. Topics of recent discussion threads included 'Brown people are still invading' and 'I am sorry but only white people are Canadian.' University campuses have also seen a rise in right wing, white supremacist and Islamophobic propaganda. Canadians do not need to look south of the border for the impetus for Islamophobic violence since it's already in our backyard.

Jasmine Zine further wrote that though Canadian and Quebecers express feelings of grief and support after the mosque attack, yet Quebec National Assembly, after just observing a minute of silence, went into discussion of Bill 62, about banning veiled women from giving or receiving government services – such discourses and policies, which sow the seeds of hate and fear, and created the perfect setting for the horrible act of terror in the mosque shooting were back in play immediately after the 60 seconds of silence.

CHAPTER 8
REMEDIES BEING WORKED TO CURB ISLAMOPHOBIA

*"And spend of your substance in the cause of Allah, and make
not your own hands contribute to (your) destruction; but do good;
for Allah loveth those who do good."*
—*The Holy Qur'an 2:195*

I am reproducing an article, 'Community needs open discussion on Islamophobia', that I wrote for Muslim Link, a community paper based in Ottawa.

Islamophobia is a serious issue affecting the Muslim community and its impact is growing day by day. How do we deal with it as a community? It is a big question.

I had the pleasure of meeting Justin Trudeau in Labrador City on April 25, 2013 at an event attended by about 200 people and I asked him this question. Mr. Trudeau provided a fairly elaborate response (about 15 minutes). Pointing to me, he acknowledged that such negative portrayals hurt and said I was courageous to proclaim I was Muslim.

My question: *When criminals commit an act of violence or terror, and if such an act is committed by a Muslim, the media loves to get into a "hyperactive" mode and indulges in a hate campaign blaming Islam, which is a false notion and contrary to what Islam teaches and promotes. Such hate campaigns are not at all conducive and they certainly promote hatred of Islam, including hate crimes. In the public interest, I feel there is a need for some legislation to control the media from fermenting such hatred. Would your party look into promoting such legislation?*

Figure 1 - *Justin Trudeau and the author with his friends and family*

Key points from his response: *Canada is home to many different types of people. It is not fair to judge anyone by religion or race. It is a fact that hate speech is often committed however I don't think the solution is to limit freedom of speech. I would prefer that it stay in the public sphere rather than in private conversation because then we can deal with the mis-understanding as a community. We have to work together because that's what Canada is about. Just because someone who committed a violent act happens to be a Muslim doesn't make Muslims bad people, in just the same way that a man who beats his wife and happens to be Christian doesn't make Christians bad people.*

I discussed this issue with Mohammed Azhar Ali Khan, well known journalist and retired judge, and he responded, "I think you expressed a legitimate concern which most Muslims share. But I agree with Justin Trudeau. Hate speech is already covered in the Criminal Code ... curbing freedom of expression is very dangerous and would turn Canada into an authoritarian society. It would help if Muslims were more pro-active in offering their views to editors, media and the politicians." He continued, "As the VIA Rail plan shows, Muslims are very vulnerable, face difficulties and would face vastly more difficult situations if such activities continue. The answer lies in trying to uplift our vulnerable members (including youth and mentally ill) and build bridges and good relations with Canadians of other faiths. This is what the Muslim community needs to do and do it together."

As a community we have to seriously deal with Islamophobia. At I.LEAD we commenced with a humble thought: to have lectures/ workshops and begin to deal with this issue.

Figure 2 - The author with Justin Trudeau

In October 2016, a 38-year-old man vandalized the Muslim cultural centre in Sept-Iles, Québec. This prompted the President of the Canadian Muslim Forum, Samer Majzoub, to reintroduce an anti-Islamophobia motion in the Parliament. Majzoub was the initiator of a Parliamentary petition against Islamophobia, which got over 70,000 signatures and ultimately inspired a Parliamentary motion on 26 October, 2016. The petition stated:

- Islam is a religion of over 1.5 billion people worldwide. Since its founding more than 1400 years ago, Muslims have contributed, and continue to contribute, to the positive development of human civilization. This encompasses all areas of human endeavours including the arts, culture, science, medicine, literature, and much more;

- Recently an infinitesimally small number of extremist individuals have conducted terrorist activities while claiming to speak for the religion of Islam. Their actions have been used as a pretext for a notable rise of anti-Muslim sentiments in Canada; and
- These violent individuals do not reflect in any way the values or the teachings of the religion of Islam. In fact, they misrepresent the religion. We categorically reject all their activities. They in no way represent the religion, the beliefs and the desire of Muslims to co-exist in peace with all peoples of the world.

We, the undersigned, **Citizens and residents of Canada**, call upon the **House of Commons** to join us in recognizing that extremist individuals do not represent the religion of Islam, and in condemning all forms of Islamophobia.

Thomas Woodley, President of Canadians for Justice and Peace in the Middle East (CJPME) wrote in an article, "While you won't find any coverage of the anti-Islamophobia motion that passed on Oct. 26 (2016), you will find articles about a similar motion that was defeated on Oct. 6.

Personally, I find it curious that a motion condemning Islamophobia that fails is news, while an identical motion that passes is not... ...This may be a case of "anti-Islamophobia motion meets Islamophobic media.""[19]

In December 2016, MPP Nathalie Des Rosiers introduced a motion in the Ontario Legislature which was helpful in combating Islamophobia. In an email dated 13 December 2016, MPP Yasir Naqvi wrote:

I wanted to share with you that MPP Nathalie Des Rosiers (Ottawa–Vanier) introduced a motion in the Ontario Legislature to reaffirm the Ontario Liberal Caucus' commitment to fighting against hatred, discrimination, and prejudices, specifically in the rise of anti-Islamic rhetoric, and recognizing the importance of diversity as part of Ontario's culture and heritage.

The motion calls to "reaffirm that diversity has always played an important part in Ontario's culture and heritage; recognizes the significant contributions Muslims have made, and continue to make, to Ontario's cultural and social fabric and prosperity; stands against all forms of hatred, hostility, prejudice, racism and intolerance; rebukes the notable growing tide of anti-Muslim rhetoric and sentiments; denounces hate-attacks, threats of violence and hate crimes against people of the Muslim faith; condemns all forms of Islamophobia and reaffirms the government's efforts through the Anti-Racism Directorate to address and prevent systemic racism in all forms across government policy, programs and services, and increase anti-racism education and awareness, including Islamophobia, in all parts of the province."

As part of her statement, Des Rosiers said, "Just last month, there were a series of attacks on religious places of worship in Ottawa, which is unacceptable in our society ... my colleagues and I are committed to fighting against all forms of hatred, hostility, prejudice, racism and intolerance. That's why it was important for me to bring forward this motion."

This October, the Ontario Legislature proclaimed October as Islamic Heritage Month in Ontario. This reiterates Ontario's commitment to embracing diversity and allows Ontarians an opportunity to celebrate and educate future generations about the important contributions

Muslim Canadians have made in their communities across the province.

This motion comes at a time when the provincial government has recognized the growing importance of addressing systemic racism, including Islamophobia, through the Anti-Racism Directorate, which was formed earlier this year in order to build a fair society and open government that is transparent, accessible and accountable to the public.

The motion combating Islamophobia was passed in February 2017. In an email dated 23 February 2017, Naqvi wrote:

I am proud to share with you that today the Ontario Legislature unanimously voted in favour of MPP Nathalie Des Rosiers' motion condemning Islamophobia.

Diversity has always played an important part in Ontario's culture and heritage. Today's motion reaffirmed that all MPPs are committed to fight against Islamophobia and all forms of discrimination that fuels acts of hatred within our society. We stand against all forms of hatred, hostility, prejudice, racism and intolerance. We also rebuke the notable growing tide of anti-Muslim rhetoric and sentiments; denounce hate-attacks, threats of violence and hate crimes against people of the Muslim faith; condemn all forms of Islamophobia and reaffirm support for government's efforts, through the Anti-Racism Directorate, to address and prevent systemic racism across government policy, programs and services, and increase anti-racism education and awareness, including Islamophobia, in all parts of the province.

We believe that hate crimes have no place in Canadian society. We take pride in the progressive and multicultural fabric of our society. Recently, the debate on a similar federal Motion denouncing Islamophobia has uprooted a number of troubling comments from the Conservative Party of Canada, which seem designed to divide and detract from the purpose of fighting discrimination.

Islamophobia needs to be addressed head on as we have seen too many acts of hatred and violence, most recently the mass shooting at the Quebec Islamic Cultural Centre in Quebec City, where six Canadians of Muslim faith were killed and 19 injured.

In light of these recent events, I, as the Government House Leader worked closely with Ottawa-Vanier MPP Nathalie Des Rosiers to move up the debate slot for this motion to the earliest opportunity when the House returns – that was today!

Today is truly a proud day for me, my family, our community and every citizen of this province. In a unanimous, 81-0 vote, all Ontario MPPs stood up against hate and discrimination.

In mid-February 2017, Member of Parliament Iqra Khalid introduced motion **M-103** calling the Canadian Parliament to condemn all forms of systemic racism and religious discrimination including Islamophobia. The motion also called for studies by HOC standing committee for Canadian Heritage on how to address the problem of religious discrimination in Canada, and how to combat religious discrimination (including Islamophobia.) Ms. Khalid received thousands of death threats, sexist comments and Islamophobic remarks after introducing M-103. The motion was successfully passed in March 2017 by a vote of 201-91.

In February 2017, I wrote an email to Chandra Arya, Member of Parliament representing my riding of Nepean, Ontario, congratulating his government for introducing M-103. I received a reply from him stating that he is a strong supporter of M-103 and provided me with the condensed text of his speech in Parliament. The full text of Arya's speech in HOC on 17 February 2017 (publicly available on Parliament's website) is as follows:

> Madam Speaker, the recent killing of Muslims praying in the mosque in Quebec City is no accident. This is the direct result of the dog-whistle politics, the politics of fear and division. Things like Muslim ban in other countries should be of concern to us. Fear is a dangerous thing. Once it is sanctioned by the state, there is no telling where it might lead. It is always a short path to walk from being suspicious of our fellow citizens to taking actions to restrict their liberty. In Canada, the elements who championed Charter values, niqab ban, barbaric cultural practices tip line, all targeted at Canadian Muslims, these elements are getting active again. It is painful and fearful to watch politicians who, in their attempts to grab power, go back to practicing the dangerous politics of fear and division.

On 16 April 2017, I forwarded a *Huffington Post* article 'Is There a Correlation between Sanctions and the Rise of Terrorism?' to Prime Minister Justin Trudeau, which tries to establish correlation between sanctions and terrorism. The article's text is reproduced in the introduction of this book. As wars add fuel to the burning fire of terrorism and thereby promote Islamophobia and could even herald the destruction of earth by trigger-happy leaders sitting on piles of nuclear weapons – I requested Justin Trudeau to use his charismatic position to influence and bring about peace in the warring world. Shortly after, on 24 April 2017, M. Bredeson (Executive Correspondence Officer for the Prime Minister's office) acknowledged the receipt of my "message of peace" and assured that my comments have been duly noted and appreciated, and that the Prime Minister, on a daily basis, is advised of the opinions offered and issues raised by Canadians in their correspondence.

It is reassuring that we have leaders in Canada who are open and opposed to Islamophobia though the likes of Harper and his syndicates were not so. They played the ugly game of divisive politics. The Liberals seem to be working to curb the rising tide of Islamophobia.

CHAPTER 9
WE MUSLIMS HAVE TO CORRECT OURSELVES TO REMEDY ISLAMOPHOBIA

"Verily, Allah will not change the (good) condition of a people as long as they do not change their state (of goodness) themselves (by committing sins and by being ungrateful and disobedient to Allah)"
—*The Holy Qur'an 13:11*

Journalist Azhar Ali Khan, wrote in the *Ottawa Citizen*: "One could list the many cases of Islamophobia in Canada: the verbal and even physical attacks on Muslims; the brick-throwing at mosques; the security laws that target mainly Muslims; the role of Canadian security authorities in the torture of Maher Arar, Abdullah Al Malki, Muayyed Nureddin and Ahmad El-Maati; the efforts by the Parti Québécois to marginalize Muslims; and even former Prime Minister Stephen Harper's efforts to demonize Muslims. Some 10 per cent of Canadians are described by polls as being racist. Muslims, and other rights advocates, including Independent Jewish Voices, are urging that action be taken to combat Islamophobia."

Khan states that, "Even so, Canadian Muslims enjoy rights and security that can only be the envy of many in most other countries, including Muslim ones."

Canadian Muslims have to make changes in their attitudes to remedy the current climate of hate against Islam. Khan says, "Canadian Muslims also need to readjust their priorities. They have been building mosques and providing mostly religious sessions. They have not devoted equal effort to building the community. Many Canadian Muslim youths came from war-torn countries and are vulnerable to drugs, alcohol, crime or extremism. These ruin their lives and if some youth commit violence that kills innocent people, the entire community could face severe consequences."

Khan points out that "many Muslim organizations also do not work together – with Shias, women and youth for example – to build the community, mould youth into becoming productive citizens and build close ties with all Canadians promoting human rights, opportunities and justice for all."

Muhammad Asad in his book *Islam at the Crossroads* provides an insightful historic reason that hatred of Islam and Muslims in modern Europe has its deep roots in the Crusades. He continues to say that, "The destruction of Muslim Spain took centuries to be accomplished. But precisely for the reason of the long duration of this fight, the anti-Islamic feeling of Europe deepened and grew to permanency."

So, what can we do as Muslims so that we are not hated? Muslims have to correct ourselves first before finding fault with others. Asad states:

> I realized that the one and only reason for the social and cultural decay of the Muslims consisted in the fact that they had gradually ceased to follow the teachings of Islam in spirit. Islam was still there; but it was a body without soul. The very element which once had stood for the strength of Muslim world was now responsible for its weakness; Islamic society has been built, from the very outset, on religious foundations alone, and the weakening of the foundations has necessarily weakened the cultural structure ... that Islam as a spiritual and social

phenomenon, is still, in spite of all the drawbacks caused by the deficiencies of the Muslims, by far the greatest driving force mankind has ever experienced.

Asad describes the *Sunnah* as "the key to the understanding of Islamic rise more than thirteen centuries ago; and why should not it be a key to the understanding of the present degeneration?" He explains that "observance of the *Sunnah* was synonymous with Islamic existence and progress. Neglect of the *Sunnah* is synonymous with decomposition and decay of Islam." *Sunnah* is "the example the Prophet has set before us in his actions and sayings. His wonderful life was a living illustration and explanation of the Qur'an, and we can do no greater justice to the Holy Book than by following him who was the means of its revelation."

The Qur'an requires that Muslims should be like a "solid building" – Asad says, "Freed from dialectical confusion and built on the solid pedestal of Divine Law and life example of our Prophet, Islamic society could use all its forces on problems of real material and intellectual welfare, thus paving the way for the individual in his spiritual endeavor. This, and nothing else, is the real religious objective of the Islamic social organization."

Asad points out:

> No doubt Islamic culture has had its splendid rise and its blossoming age, it had power to inspire men to deeds and sacrifices, it transformed nations and changed the face of earth; and later it stood still and became stagnant, and then it became an empty word, and at present we witness its utter debasement and decay ... What appears to be the decay of Islam is in reality nothing but the death of our hearts which are too idle and too lazy to hear the eternal voice. No sign is visible that mankind, in its present stature, has outgrown Islam. It has not been

able to put the idea of human brotherhood on a practical footing, as Islam did in its supra-national concept of 'ummah' (Islamic nation), it has not been able to create a social structure in which conflicts and frictions between its members are as efficiently reduced to a minimum as in the social plan of Islam; it has not been able to enhance the dignity of man; his feeling of security; his spiritual hope; and last, but surely not the least, his happiness.

Muslims should be like a "solid building". But, unfortunately, many of us are not like that. We fight amongst ourselves and, in the process, end up ruining good things. As an example, I would like to share a personal anecdote. In late 2011, I invited a number of local Muslim community leaders to my residence. Over dinner, I proposed that there was a need in Ottawa for a large-scale community event with the purpose of teaching Islamic guidance. There were several mosques in the city, but they all operated independently and seldom did they organize events by pooling their resources together. What was being proposed was to organize a conference by a unified front.

Myself and a handful of other dedicated volunteers initiated a conference called I.LEAD (Islam: Lead, Engage, Achieve, Develop) built on the concept of unity. Several mosques in Ottawa and the neighbouring city of Gatineau joined together in a unique collaboration—two or three coming together has happened before and is rare enough, let alone a collaboration of eleven. The conference was a success, so it became an annual event. In the words of Prime Minister Justin Trudeau in 2016, "This year's conference marks the fourth I.LEAD, which is well-known for its positive atmosphere and inclusive discussions with the intention of creating a better world for all to live in."

The success of I.LEAD was not without its challenges. With its growing success, some perceived that I was trying to make I.LEAD an organization independent of the mosques. But the intent of I.LEAD from the beginning was to be a platform on which the mosques could unify, not to supersede them. It was also perceived that I wanted to maintain sole control of I.LEAD. At the end of every conference, I offered to step down from my role, but I was repeatedly asked by the majority to remain. I dedicated my time to this volunteer role as if it were a full-time job, simply because I believed in the vision of a unified community, not because I wanted power.

Unfortunately, following the fourth conference, I was ousted from my role as chairperson due to an unfairly conducted election. The reason given was to bring new blood into the conference organizing committee. While we certainly do need to give opportunity for people to learn and develop as leaders so that an organization can last beyond its founding members, I do believe that there is a process by which this should occur. One does not hand the role of CEO of a company over to just any person. Such a person has to be trained and given time to learn from others who have more experience. So unfortunately, the reason given for pushing me out of the committee was on flimsy grounds.

It seems to me that the real reason for the ousting was that there was a power grab. I.LEAD was growing in success and certain people wanted to take hold of it. The infighting that occurred compromised the foundations that the conference was built on. I believe that this is a case in point of Asad's diagnosis of the Muslim community. We may start off with good intentions, but we often fall short of following Islamic guidance in our lives. In this example, the shortfall was in how to resolve conflict, maintaining good intentions, and avoiding egoistic tendencies for power—all of these are issues that Islam offers guidance on. Regrettably, this episode resulted in me being removed from the picture unjustly. I use this example here only because I want to speak up and break the silence on what is happening in our Muslim communities.

Speaking much more broadly at the Muslim states level, there are also bloodthirsty *Shia/Sunni* fights. Muslim/Muslim fights seem to be the norm of the day. If we correct ourselves and live by the *Sunnah* of the holy Prophet (peace be upon him) by following his conduct and his spirit, we would not be as despised and hated as we are now. It was not an ordinary feat that in just 80 years the immediate followers of the holy Prophet (peace be upon him) took the light of Islam to the four corners of earth, to three known continents and shaped the Muslim empire to its peak. The glory continued for 1000 years. Only later was there a gradual decline owing to the loss of Islamic spirit.

CHAPTER 10
SAY NO TO ISLAMOPHOBIA

*"And the servants of the Most Merciful are those who walk
upon the earth easily, and when the ignorant address them [harshly],
they say [words of] peace"*
—The Holy Qur'an 25:63

At the time of first Gulf War in early 1991, we were in Dammam-Khobar, which was part of the war zone – most of the twin towns were empty as people had evacuated. We saw the Scud missiles from Iraq zooming in and Patriot missiles chasing them to defend. Towards the end of the war, a Scud made its way and landed right on a US army camp killing and wounding a number of US soldiers – that location was less than a few kilometres from our residence. It really rattled the doors and windows. With the wailing of sirens, initially, we used to retreat to an airtight room of our residence with our gas masks on. Later, we realized that those masks were not necessary, and it was just hype! My youngest son, Bassam, was two years old and I still remember how emotional he used to get with the sound of siren – he would say, *"Mummy, bam pada, thath hoi* (Mummy, bomb fell and *thath* happened – *"thath"* was the sound when the scud made a hit*), all clear!"*

Naturally, I started following the war, its destruction and the aftermath including the sanctions and other Middle East wars. I was sure in my mind that the law of Physics which states, "Every action has an equal and opposite reaction" would literally hold good in a sense that those affected by the war would react irrationally too and all that going around will come around to haunt the West!

In 1994, we immigrated to Canada and got a chance to work with the group that was opposing the sanctions. With the passage of time, terrorism started growing at a tremendous speed. I was following articles – though not much reported in the mainstream media – about the wars and sanctions. All the references and links that I have provided in this book are very close to my own thinking. Arabs and Muslims were associated with quite a few terrorist attacks – I don't endorse nor does Islam promote or endorse violence that kills innocent people. The compassionate laws of wars are well defined in Islam. The growing terrorism has given rise to Islamophobia at an alarming rate.

Islamophobia, makes me think, in fact, I am sure it comes to your mind too, is something wrong with Islam or Muslims? Muhammad Asad's thinking in *Islam at the Crossroads* is in perfect tune with my thinking that Muslims have forgotten the real teachings of Islam, and we are Muslims only for namesake and not in spirit at all – how true he is when he wrote the book decades ago.

Our, five times a day, obligatory prayer has become a ritual, forgetting the real purpose that it is meant to bring us closer to the Creator, obey Him and not to disobey Him. Where is the all submissive *sajda* (prostration) of the *sahaba* (companions of the holy Prophet) – a poet rightly points out:

> *"Woh sajda roohe zamin jis se kanp jati thi*
> *Usiko aaj taraste hain mimbar wo mihrab"*

> *Where is the sajda (prostration), with which the soul of the earth used to tremble?*
> *Pulpit and niche are pleading for that sajda (prostration)*

Following verses and commands from the Holy Qur'an come to mind to show us clearly as to how we should act and how we should improve as Muslims.

In *Surah Al-Asr,* Allah (swt) swears by the declining day and says to the effect that humans are at loss except those who believe and do righteous deeds, and exhort one another to truth and patience. Imam Shaf'ai has said this *Surah* is enough if we ponder on it.

Qur'an clearly commands to the effect, "O people of Dawood (peace be upon him), do acts to thank." Thanking the Creator of course begins with thanking humans for their acts of kindness.

Qur'an also states that they (the prophets) hastened to do righteous deeds.

Surah At-Theen states that Man has been created in the best of the mould but he goes down to the lowest of low except those who believe and do righteous deeds.

Again from the Qur'an, we are the best nation brought out for people to command right and prevent wrong.

Further, the Qur'an states that death and life after death have been created to test that we do righteous deeds.

Qur'an says that *jinn* and men have been created except to worship. Worship is a 24/7 activity and does not consist of just performing the five obligatory prayers but in a broad sense, it means to obey and get closer to the Creator.

In short, we have to revive our spirit, perform righteous deeds, get out of stagnation and not gather moss like still water. We need to flow like water – gush like a swift flowing stream or a cascading waterfall, giving all the best to the world that we could and all the good will come back to us. In fact, it is said in a *hadith* that *deen* (faith) is easy like water (and it certainly benefits). Let us remove the Islamophobia, and say, no to terrorism!

CHAPTER 11
SPEAK UP, BREAK THE SILENCE

*"Invite to the way of your Lord with wisdom and good instruction,
and argue with them in a way that is best. Indeed, your Lord is
most knowing of who has strayed from His way, and He is most
knowing of who is [rightly] guided."*
—The Holy Qur'an 16:125

Whether it is childhood abuse, atrocities against a country, or any situation that demands the broken silence of the good people watching from the sidelines, people should speak up. Otherwise it will end up normalizing the abuse – this is really important. Abuse hurts, wrongs are painful, injustice destroys!

Personally, I think, I take negatives and try to turn them into positives, and I do realize that most people who have experienced something similar may or may not be able to turn things around and show similar resilience. But speaking up is not easy, it requires courage of conviction. I was meek, I was silent but gradually built up that courage to speak out, speak out against wrong. For Muslim youth or for anybody, the life of the holy Prophet (*peace be upon him*) is the finest example to follow. Or even choose the life of any of the companions of the holy Prophet (*peace be upon him*) who are like shining stars. If we follow them, we are guided and we can build up that courage of conviction. The world has produced many courageous people, and we should get inspired by them.

To whom we should speak or speak out against: it depends. I have seen that problems are generally resolved, wrongs are righted when we politely 'confront' the person with truth – ask them why they did it; they may apologize and even if they don't we can at least vent out our feelings and such 'encounters' do clear up the ill feelings.

We often see that wrongs are done to us by many, including service organizations, for example, it could be an airline or a hotel. I don't ignore wrongs but I 'confront' them with a letter and often I have seen that it produces some results, such as an apology and sometimes even a little compensation. Wrongs are committed in the course of employment by the employers too. Resist, fight back, don't give up but be polite, and don't lose your cool.

We come across injustice and wrong at a massive level – at both personal level and public level, and it becomes necessary that we pursue legal action or mass action but that may not be an easy task due to lack of resources or lack of support or lack of organization. I have often felt and wished that I could mobilize support and form a group that would have the courage of conviction and resources to demand justice, and right the wrong not only at a personal level but at a public level too. Having said that, if like-minded readers come forward to volunteer such efforts, I am very much willing to be part of such a group, such an effort – they will enjoin right and forbid wrong. For sure, together, we could do it, God willing!

Now that I am looking at a future where my life stories, particularly of abuse, are out for everyone to read – it will be an honour if it could help others to realize the abuse they might have gone through in their lives. It's OK to speak up. There is nothing to be ashamed of. I encourage readers to speak up and not stand watching from the sidelines – be it in the form of letters to the government or through forming a conference or organization. People might try to destroy what you have painstakingly built over the years but I believe that when you give the best to the world, you will get back better than that. So speak up, break the silence!

ENDNOTES

1 https://www.un.org/Depts/unmovic/documents/687.pdf

2 http://www.casi.org.uk/info/garfield/dr-garfield.html

3 https://www.ncbi.nlm.nih.gov/pmc/articles/PMC1120689/

4 https://www.ourcommons.ca/DocumentViewer/en/37-1/house/sitting-59/hansard

5 https://georgewbush-whitehouse.archives.gov/news/releases/2003/03/20030322.html

6 https://www.democracynow.org/2015/3/2/noam_chomsky_on_how_the_iraq

7 https://www.thenation.com/article/what-i-discovered-from-interviewing-isis-prisoners/

8 https://www.tandfonline.com/doi/abs/10.1080/03050629.2013.768478

9 https://www.counterpunch.org/2016/12/01/petraeus-redux/

10 https://www.counterpunch.org/2017/02/13/trump-will-ignite-a-war-with-iran-which-will-be-great-news-for-isis/

11 https://www.counterpunch.org/2017/02/14/worst-joke-ever-u-s-spy-chief-gives-saudi-prince-highest-award-for-fighting-terrorism/

12 https://www.counterpunch.org/2017/05/29/no-laughing-matter-the-manchester-bomber-is-the-spawn-of-hillary-and-baracks-excellent-libyan-adventure/

13 https://www.counterpunch.org/2016/09/28/donald-trump-islamophobia-and-immigrants/

14   https://www.counterpunch.org/2017/02/17/
     why-trumps-muslim-travel-ban/

15   http://poll.forumresearch.com/post/2646/
     muslims-the-target-of-most-racial-bias/

16   https://www.vice.com/en_ca/article/8gkkna/new-survey-
     exposing-quebecs-islamophobia-is-just-tip-of-iceberg-muslim-
     group-says

17   https://www.environicsinstitute.org/projects/project-details/
     survey-of-muslims-in-canada-2016

18   https://irdproject.com/quebec-massacre-home-grown-islam-
     ophobia-white-supremacist-nationalism-great-white-north/

19   https://www.huffingtonpost.ca/thomas-woodley/canada-anti-
     islamophobia-law_b_12753924.html

CPSIA information can be obtained
at www.ICGtesting.com
Printed in the USA
LVHW050455261119
638500LV00006B/436/P